Reflecting realities

Participants' perspectives on integrated communities and sustainable development

Jean Anastacio, Ben Gidley, Lorraine Hart, Michael Keith,
Marjorie Mayo and Ute Kowarzik

First published in Great Britain in July 2000 by

The Policy Press
34 Tyndall's Park Road
Bristol BS8 1PY
UK

Tel no +44 (0)117 954 6800
Fax no +44 (0)117 973 7308
E-mail tpp@bristol.ac.uk
www.policypress.org.uk

Published for the Joseph Rowntree Foundation by The Policy Press

ISBN 1 86134 270 5

Jean Anastacio is Lecturer, **Michael Keith** is Professor of Sociology, **Marjorie Mayo** is Reader in Community Development, **Ben Gidley** and **Ute Kowarzik** are both researchers in the Centre for Urban and Community Research, all at Goldsmiths College, University of London. **Lorraine Hart** is a consultant based at the Environment Trust.

The **Joseph Rowntree Foundation** has supported this project as part of its programme of research and innovative development projects, which it hopes will be of value to policy makers, practitioners and service users. The facts presented and views expressed in this report are, however, those of the authors and not necessarily those of the Foundation.

Cover design by Qube Design Associates, Bristol
Front cover: right photograph kindly supplied by Paul Halliday; left photograph kindly supplied by www.johnbirdsall.co.uk
Printed in Great Britain by Hobbs the Printers Ltd, Southampton

Contents

Acknowledgements

We are extremely grateful for the extraordinary amount of help and cooperation that we received from community representatives and activists, professionals and decision makers in each of the case study locations. We are also extremely grateful for the help and advice offered to the research by the Advisory Group that met regularly throughout the project under the auspices of the Joseph Rowntree Foundation. The Advisory Group made many useful and timely contributions to our work.

A number of colleagues made valuable comments on the draft report. We would like to thank them most warmly for their help and advice. Any remaining errors are, of course, our own.

Also, thanks for administrative support go to Ginna Nyarko, Angela Kerkhoff and Pamela Wallis.

Jean Anastacio
Ben Gidley
Lorraine Hart
Michael Keith
Ute Kowarzik
Marjorie Mayo

In collaboration with the Audit Tool Team:
Danny Burns and Marilyn Taylor

Introduction

Aims of the project and the report

This project set out to explore communities' own views about their experiences of small area regeneration programmes. The aims were:

- To explore participants' perspectives on the lessons to be learnt from their experiences of participation in area regeneration programmes, for building integrated, sustainable and democratically accountable structures for community participation.
- To explore participants' perspectives on the lessons for providing effective and appropriate support, including technical resources, skills training and learning in community participation.
- To explore participants' perspectives on the impact of their involvement through monitoring and evaluation mechanisms; and to explore what lessons can be drawn for participatory approaches to community involvement in monitoring and evaluation.
- To explore how far participants' perspectives varied, taking account of diversity in terms of factors such as ethnicity, gender, occupation and age.
- To develop audit tools for communities, professionals and decision makers to monitor and evaluate structures and support mechanisms to facilitate effective community participation.

Original contribution

Across a wide range of social and economic policy initiatives the value and significance of 'community participation' is increasingly stressed. Throughout the 1990s innovations in community participation were piloted in area regeneration programmes, as well as in other social and economic policy fields. This widespread acceptance of the need for community participation in the processes of regeneration has evinced in a number of good practice guidelines. Despite these positive moves, there is continuing evidence of considerable depths of dissatisfaction from among the very communities that are being represented and 'regenerated'.

The reasons for this mismatch between rhetoric and reality are complex. Despite the evident shortcomings, there *are* also examples of good practice. The possibilities for change and the constraints within which change operates are both explored through the varied experiences examined in this report.

This study starts from the position that for community participation to be effective, it is essential for regenerators to understand:

- the pluralities and diversity of community interests;
- the complexities of 'representation' and 'democratic accountability' and not reducing community participation to a parody of the formal electoral process;
- the two-way relationships between 'communities' and regeneration initiatives: 'communities' are in part defined by regeneration initiatives just as they, in part, define their needs in response to the presence of regeneration agencies;
- and build effective two-way relationships between small area programmes and mainstream policy programmes at local, regional and national levels.

While this report focuses on community participation in area regeneration programmes, the issues have key relevance for a range of contemporary policy agendas. In particular, both the local government reform agenda and the new requirements of Best Value demand that local authorities take forward processes of community participation through the production of community plans for local areas. A sophisticated understanding of the dynamics of community life is necessary for this to occur effectively. In particular the statuses of different associations, networks and institutions need to be reflected in the composition of any community plan, taking account of underlying inequalities of power between the different sectors and stakeholders. This report speaks both about the nature of such complexity and to the processes that might be adopted in composing such plans, including the use of audit tools to monitor and evaluate processes of community participation.

Topicality

Three areas of contemporary social policy debate are particularly relevant to the focus of this report:

- Holistic social policy, social inclusion and lifelong learning for active citizenship.
- New 'local' and small area policies and their relationships to regional structures.
- The legitimacy of governance: accountability, representation and stakeholder democracy.

Holistic social policy, social inclusion and lifelong learning for active citizenship

A key feature of social policy concerns in many affluent societies has been the degree to which different departments of government coordinate their work. In the British context, there has been an increasing focus on the *impact* of employment and training, crime prevention, health and social welfare policies – the degree to which finite resources are being effectively targeted at those in most need and the degree to which local communities are simultaneously the *recipients of* and *participants in* particular forms of 'joined-up' government.

Area regeneration programmes are being challenged to demonstrate their validity as tools of change that benefit, and work in active partnerships with, communities characterised by concentrations of social and economic deprivation. Historically, debates have been couched in terms of an ultimately limited contrast between 'top-down' and 'bottom-up' approaches to regeneration. This report highlights the case for displacing this couplet of terms, focusing instead on the inter-relationships between social policies (as these are developed and implemented at national, regional and local levels) and the populations and geographical areas that these policies are intended to serve.

Regeneration structures create new forms of resource allocation and new modes of community participation in structures of governance. These new forms of community participation have been advocated, both for their contribution to specific regeneration initiatives, and for their contribution to the development of 'social capital' in the longer-term. 'Social capital' has been defined and valued in two ways that have specific relevance here: as 'bonding capital' – meaning networks and relationships of trust within communities; and as 'bridging capital' – meaning the networks and inter-relationships between communities and external organisations and agencies, including those with key powers and resources. The Social Exclusion Unit, for example, has emphasised the importance of building 'social capital' in both senses of the term, and this has been a significant factor in the thinking behind the New Deal for Communities (see particularly, SEU, 1999a, 1999b, 1999c, 1999d).

The development of social capital also has considerable relevance for debates on lifelong learning and learning for active citizenship. Individuals and groups learn in significant ways from their experiences of participating in area regeneration programmes as active citizens. There are important benefits here, both for the individuals and the organisations concerned.

Small area regeneration programmes also highlight a number of problems associated with the generation of such networks of social capital. Social capital, like any other form of capital, represents a key resource for those who have access to it. The acquisition of social capital by some – the 'community stars' – may actually be to the detriment of others – particularly to the detriment of groups already struggling with social exclusion on the basis of race, gender, occupation or age.

By definition, an effective community network reconfigures power structures, both *within* communities and *between* community networks and wider power structures and resources, in both public and private sectors. But in the exercise of representing 'the community' such a network is also by definition partial – networks are not typically based on the active participation of all their potential constituents in the community. Ironically, as this report demonstrates in the following section, this partial status can actually be used against the network itself (when decision makers rationalise their reluctance to take particular issues seriously, for example, on the grounds that the case is being put forward by an 'unrepresentative group'). This makes it all the more important for these issues of representation and democratic accountability to be effectively addressed, and for the benefits of learning for active citizenship to be made available inclusively. The notion of community participation needs to be understood as a continuing process of learning and *dialogue* between all those concerned – between the structures of governance and local people, in communities that are in part defined precisely by the boundaries of the Single Regeneration Budget (SRB) area, the Employment Zone or the Health Action Zone. (The bidding guidelines for New Deal for Communities, Health and Education Action Zones and SRB rounds 1-6 have increasingly come to acknowledge both the significance of community involvement in area regeneration programmes, the difficulties with existing and past models of participation and the need to redress these flaws in the future.)

New 'local' and small area policies and their relationships to regional structures

The notion that the nation state has become 'too small to do the big things and too large to do the small things' has focused interest on the *local* level in a wide range of social policy areas. From a focus on regions and regional development through to Health Action Zones, New Deal for Communities, New Deal for Employment, Employment Zones, Surestart and Education Action Zones, a series of policy measures focus attention on the geographical scales on which these different strands of social policy are delivered.

The complexity of modern society might appear to challenge the analytical value of the notion of community. There have been rapid changes associated with industrialisation, deindustrialisation and migration. The notion of community has also been complicated by the growing significance of alternative sentiments of identity politics (alongside longstanding class solidarities). These changes necessitate a subtler understanding of the manner in which the imagining of communities becomes meaningful for people at different times, in different places and in different policy contexts.

The changing policy context has particular relevance for this study. For example 'communities' based primarily on residence in local authority housing estates have been significantly affected by the degree of the *residualisation* of social housing. Policies over the last two decades have produced a double residualisation of the local authority social landlord function. In London and the South East in particular, the reduced levels of stock caused by Right to Buy legislation in the early 1980s have 'creamed off' much of the most desirable social housing. Housing stock transfers are likewise geared towards the more 'desirable' estates, because of local authorities' need to raise finance on their value. The end result has been the increasing residualisation of social housing, with increasing concentrations of social deprivation in the remaining residue. In parallel, as case studies in this report illustrate, the tenants' movement has also suffered from increasing marginalisation from the mainstream of community representation structures. These processes will not be resolved by community development strategies within neighbourhoods alone.

As the findings illustrate, the implications for addressing the problems of social exclusion go way beyond the confines of the neighbourhoods in question, raising issues for social policy nationally and regionally, taking account of the new regional structures. Part of the policy relevance of this report lies in these wider implications for the ways in which we think about 'communities' and 'community participation'. In the present policy context, if communities are to participate in addressing the causes of social exclusion, there need to be effective frameworks for dialogue which go way beyond the level of the locality. The new regional structures could be key in this regard (positively or negatively), opening up or closing off essential communication channels.

Before leaving these issues associated with changing concepts of 'community', two key normative terms which structured our thinking in this research need to be clarified. The first is the notion of 'integrated communities'. By this we were absolutely not implying that communities are – or should be – integrated as homogenous entities. On the contrary, communities are characterised by diversity and difference, and this applies both to geographical communities and to communities based on ethnicity or shared interest or identity. The key issue for our research was whether or not communities were 'integrated' in the sense that these diverse interests were being represented effectively and *inclusively*. Were all these different voices being heard, or only the most powerful or the most vocal? And were these diverse interests able to collaborate – to work together in solidarity – on issues of shared concern? Were groups, organisations and agencies working in complementary ways, when they identified shared objectives, and were they effective in raising their concerns in wider policy arenas at regional levels and beyond? Was the community sector being strengthened? Or conversely, was social capital being undermined? Were groups and organisations becoming locked in conflicts, despite their common interests, as they competed for scarce resources?

The second key term was the notion of 'sustainable regeneration'. By this we were referring to regeneration programmes which build on, rather than by-pass or undermine existing strengths within and between communities, empowering them to develop their own agendas and organisational structures (including community development trusts, for example). Sustainable regeneration programmes would also be characterised by their inter-relationships with mainstream policies and programmes, and mainstream structures, including the new regional structures, ensuring improved economic, employment and social conditions in the local area and the wider region and beyond.

The legitimacy of governance: accountability, representation and stakeholder democracy

The reform of local democracy represents the third key policy area addressed by this report. A major concern for government has been the degree to which local communities recognise and participate in structures of local governance. Many of the changes that are proposed in the working of local government in Britain – notably notions of partnership, stakeholder representation and community leadership – have been piloted through area regeneration programmes such as City Challenge and SRB.

Democratic accountability is more than a matter of an annual or four-yearly electoral mandate. The democratic deficit is particularly evident in areas characterised by low turnouts at elections – an issue especially in areas characterised by high levels of deprivation and social exclusion. For democratic systems to be seen to be legitimate, there is an evident need to explore new approaches to participation and more nuanced notions of 'accountability' and 'representation'. Area regeneration programmes provide extensive evidence of both good and bad practices that can inform such a debate. Most importantly they point to more sophisticated understandings of how individuals, associations and community groups come to constitute the social and political life of cities and how best such complex patterns of community life can be represented inclusively. Critical reflections on these experiences of participation can contribute directly to the ways in which changes in local democratic structures and working practices will, or will not, revive interest in local government and the new forms of regional governance.

Research and methodology

Basic principles

The research team was concerned to gather the opinions, accounts and perceptions of those communities that had experience of small area regeneration programmes. In some important senses these narratives contrasted significantly with *official* accounts of the same programmes. Although the research drew on subjective experiences of individuals and organisations, the accumulation of material and the triangulation of accounts provided academic validity. The basic principle of the research was to draw on participatory research techniques to work through processes of dialogue with local people. The aim was to facilitate the emergence of communities' own stories. We are extremely grateful for the extraordinary amount of help and cooperation that we received in each of the case study locations. Despite the pressures, people gave of their time most generously.

Preliminary work and literature review

Before the field research took place, an extensive literature review was carried out in three phases. The first phase examined published academic work and analysed the 'grey' literature produced by policy-making institutions. The second involved a further survey of 110 urban regeneration programmes and organisations, detailing the form and degree of community participation adopted by them. The third phase widened the analysis to other social policy areas to examine the parallels in community participation in the literature on 'third' world development and in policy literatures that relate to the restructuring of the provision of social welfare services in the 'first' world. The results of this work were published in an interim report (available from CUCR, Goldsmiths College, University of London). A supplementary literature review was completed at the end of the fieldwork. This examined policy changes in relation to the government's National Strategy for Neighbourhood Renewal and for small area-based initiatives such as New Deal for Communities, Neighbourhood Management, Employment Zones, Health and Education Actions Zones, the most recent sets of SRB guidelines, the work of the Social Exclusion Unit and its Policy Action Teams.

Key findings from the literature review

The literature review started from the need to explore participants' reflections on the gap between good practice, in theory, and their experiences of practice, in reality (Taylor, 1995; Clapham, 1996; Hastings et al, 1996). Community participants' own perceptions and evaluations – of the processes as well as the outputs and outcomes of area regeneration programmes – were indeed notable for their relative absence in England and Wales. There was some evidence about the issue of sustainability (including evidence about the positive contributions of Community Development Trusts) and there were examples of publications which addressed issues of process, but even these represented a small minority of the publications reviewed. The literature on Scottish experiences of community participation in area regeneration programmes was relatively fuller, and also included specific references to participatory research methods (Hastings and MacArthur, 1995). This reinforced the team's views that gaps existed which needed to be addressed through this research in England.

The literature on participatory monitoring and evaluation in 'third world' development contexts, however, provided a range of evidence to demonstrate the potential and the value of participatory research with communities (Estrella and Gaventa, 1998). There was a range of evidence, both in written and in other formats (such as video), to illustrate the point that even people who were extremely resource-poor and/or lacking in basic literacy skills, could and did become active researchers, assessing their own needs and possibilities for sustainable development. There were examples of local people evaluating the success or otherwise of development projects. It was argued that reflection, action, monitoring and evaluation could all be linked in effective development processes on the basis of these studies.

The literature on participatory research in development contexts added two further points which were directly useful for our research. First, the literature emphasised the importance of taking adequate account of diversity and difference. This was essential if all voices – including the voices of less powerful groups, such as women, in so many contexts – were to be effectively heard (Guijt and Shah, 1998). And this literature raised critical questions about the relationships between local participatory research and the wider implications for policies at regional, national and international levels (Holland et al, 1998).

More specifically, this literature also provided illustrations of a range of tools which could be adapted for our purposes, alongside the tools to be developed via the audit tools research. These tools included the use of diagrams to plot power relations and to explore the implications for strategies for development and change. The use of participatory video was similarly discussed and evaluated.

There was also relevant evidence from the literature review of user involvement in monitoring and evaluating social welfare services. Here, there were examples to illustrate that this type of participatory research was both possible and valuable (Wilson, 1995). These examples included illustrations, working with user groups of people with learning disabilities, with ex-users of mental health services (Lindow and Morris, 1995) and with children in relation to childcare services (Cloke and Davies, 1995; Schofield and Thoburn, 1996). The literature on the participation of children and young people has been developing most significantly in recent months and years (Fitzpatrick et al, 1998).

In addition to demonstrating the potential and the relevance of this type of user involvement in monitoring and evaluation, this part of the literature review also pointed to the following factors that were particularly relevant for our research. To be effective, user involvement needed to be built into the research process throughout, starting from the research design. This needed to be based on processes of dialogue with the researchers. Rather than researchers extracting findings from users, researchers and users needed to collaborate within a more equal partnership – from which both can benefit (Barnes and Mercer, 1997). And these processes of dialogue needed to be supported and resourced.

This point was particularly relevant in the light of one of the other overall findings from the literature review – the relative lack of resourcing, including the relative lack of appropriate training for community participation in area regeneration programmes, more generally. The situation overall, it was concluded, was no more than patchy (Henderson and Mayo, 1998). The relative lack of opportunities for networking between community representatives in different areas also emerged, despite the fact that this was widely seen as valuable (Gilchrist and Taylor, 1997).

Selection of case study locations

The following criteria were developed to select the four case study areas. These criteria aimed to ensure that it would be possible to obtain as comprehensive a picture of community participants' perspectives as possible.

1. It was important to identify areas with a history of participation, including areas with relatively well-developed community infrastructures, so that communities would be in a position to reflect upon the lessons of their experiences over time and to evaluate the sustainability of past initiatives.
2. Given the intention to identify examples of good practice, it would also be important to include areas which had clearly enjoyed some positive experiences, including positive experiences of professional support and training.
3. In view of the importance attached to issues of diversity and difference, exclusion and

inclusion, it was essential to include examples of communities characterised by ethnic diversity.

4. Because of the focus on sustainability, it would also be important to include areas where issues of sustainability were being directly addressed (for example, via Community Development Trusts) and where there were examples of community-managed programmes, developed to meet communities' own definitions of their needs.
5. Given the diversity of institutional responses to community participation, it was also decided to include examples of different 'political' cultures (such as local authorities which were more-or-less sympathetic to working in partnership with communities).
6. Finally it was important to select areas which were relatively accessible both geographically and, most importantly, accessible in terms of contacts with communities, professionals and decision makers (that is, where there was potential local interest in participating in the research). This aspect took on even greater significance as the literature review confirmed the importance of participatory approaches to the research process itself, building up collaborative relationships between researchers and those whose perspectives were to be researched. Conversely it was important not to select areas which were already being extensively studied by other researchers, or suffering from research overload as a result of relatively recent studies. (Newcastle, for example, was ruled out on these grounds.)

The four sites chosen were:

- the Aston/Newtown area of Birmingham
- Barnsley in the South Yorkshire Coalfield
- the Greenwich Waterfront in South London
- Kings Cross in inner North London

In each area a nine-step methodology was followed.

1. A list of contacts was drawn up from community representative bodies in the area and other key stakeholders, such as local authority members and officers, regeneration partnership members and representatives from government regional offices.
2. The research team set out in each area to contact community members and groups that were involved in the regeneration process –

and groups that were not involved in area regeneration programmes – in each locality, in order to explore their perspectives.

3. One of the aims of our work was to generate a set of tools that could be used to audit individual regeneration programmes to identify the strengths and weaknesses of particular models of community participation. In two of the four case study locations the audit issues were discussed at this point with an invited cross-section of community representatives in an initial focus group discussion. Original focus groups were used to inform subsequent consideration of the audit tools development process.

4. Before making contact with people in each of the case study sites an extensive review of secondary literature was carried out covering area regeneration programme bidding and local delivery plans, a number of websites and other relevant background material. In each area appointments were made with between 30 and 50 individuals and organisations. The semi-structured interviews lasted between one and two hours. The list of interviewees was supplemented, in each case study, both by 'snowball' contacts and through other informal contacts in each locality. Interviews were focused on the research questions raised in the original proposal. Interviews were taped and interview material was written up and subjected to analysis using NUD.IST software (a programme for analysing qualitative data).

5. On the basis of the fieldwork and local literature reviews the research team produced what was described as a 'first cut' representation of the institutional landscape of area regeneration and a preliminary assessment of the form and nature of community participation, in each case study area. Each of the four 'first cut' descriptions was written in a non-technical 'reader-friendly' fashion, rather than as academic documents. The purpose of these 'first cut' representations was both to feed back to participants the initial findings and also to serve as the basis of further discussion. 'First cut' representations were sent back to all participants in the research process and formal comments and corrections were invited.

6. In each of the case study locations a series of between three and six focus groups were convened, bringing together individuals and organisations with similar interests. For example, in most of the case study areas, one focus group brought together officers from the local authority and regeneration partnerships while others brought together varying combinations of community interests, including focus groups comprising those whose views had not so far been effectively heard (such as young people). These focus groups were then used to check the factual historical accuracy of the 'first cut' reports and to trigger reflections on the lessons that could be learned from the regeneration process locally. This also lead to discussions about models of good practice that might be developed and disseminated. In some cases these focus groups were video taped.

7. On the basis of the focus group discussions, these accounts of community participation locally were refined further and a joint summary of the findings was drafted, based on these four local case studies.

8. Further focus groups took place in two of the case study locations specifically to explore issues that related directly to the development of the audit tools.

9. Once the findings of the project had been drafted, participants from each of the four areas were invited to joint workshops (one in Birmingham and the other in London) to reflect upon their comparative experiences. The workshop in Birmingham was held at Fircroft College. This lasted 24 hours (spread over two days) and involved representatives from all four localities. The subsequent workshop, in London, was arranged for representatives who had been unable to travel to Birmingham. This workshop was concentrated into one evening.

In conclusion, it is important to acknowledge that we believe that the use of participatory techniques was valid and extremely valuable. But we do also recognise that the research process was characterised by limitations as well as by strengths.

Strengths
•   The participatory nature of the research and the use of multi-media methods (audio tape, video tape, graphical representation) provided several avenues through which community perceptions could be represented throughout the research process.
•   The nature of comparative research facilitated important insights into those flaws that were

structural to the regeneration process and those that were locally contingent.

- The ability to draw community participants together through the research process appeared to be both beneficial to the research and useful for participants in the research.

Limitations

- Finite logistical resources meant that the research team was inevitably to a degree 'parachuting' into research contexts, gathering information and then leaving (despite the overall commitment to more participatory ways of working).
- Although the research team consciously attempted to develop contacts with those excluded from regeneration processes locally, it is important to be cautious about the degree to which this was possible, especially given the limited time available.

Case study locations

Aston/Newtown, Birmingham

Descriptive features

Aston/Newtown is a small inner-city area just north of the centre of Birmingham. In 1993 the area was awarded £37.5 million towards the second round City Challenge in Newtown/South Aston, 1993-98. As the City Challenge developed its exit strategy a voluntary and community sector partnership covering the overlapping area of Aston/Newtown was awarded regeneration funds under the 'Breaking the Cycle' Aston Birmingham SRB. The programme had total funds of £8.2 million.

This SRB's strategic aims focus in particular on issues of capacity building and training, with a strong emphasis on issues in relation to race, racism and ethnicity. Ethnic minority residents who formed 55% of the area's population were not being reached by mainstream programmes. Key outputs were to be jobs created/safeguarded, community enterprise start-ups, and training (with a particular focus on ethnic minority groups), access to finance and housing improvements.

The area is also characterised by other forms of community participation locally. Housing Liaison Boards (HLBs) are a set of structures for tenant and resident participation in relation to housing issues in Birmingham. They are city council structures that have been established over a number of years. There has also been a programme for Local Involvement and Local Action (LILA) that has been developed as part of Birmingham City Council decentralisation initiatives. These initiatives have particular relevance in Birmingham, because of the overall size of the local authority and the scale of the

Bangladeshi Youth Forum

The Bangladeshi Youth Forum (BYF) was already established by young Bangladeshi people before City Challenge came to Aston/Newtown. BYF was set up to provide services to Bangladeshi young people (including youth clubs, social activities and outings as well as training in information technologies) and to press to make existing mainstream services more appropriate and relevant.

The City Challenge boundary effectively excluded the Bangladeshi community in the neighbouring area from the benefits of City Challenge – despite the fact that their needs were just as great. BYF challenged this. Through their own efforts and sheer determination, they made their case convincingly. As a BYF member commented, BYF was so obviously providing relevant services that their 'activities spoke for themselves'. As a result of BYF's efforts, and with the support of the local community work team, BYF eventually obtained space within the City Challenge offices, and gained access to City Challenged resources.

BYF is now partner in the voluntary sector-led SRB in the area. They have a thriving centre which actively involves young women as well as young men. BYF has enabled young Bangladeshi people to voice their views, and to become active partners in the regeneration process. As one on their members commented, "We're showing results; we get on with the work", although this member went on to reflect that the views of young Bangladeshi people were still not being sufficiently heard, overall.

Commenting on BYF's achievements, a community representative from another group reflected that BYF had been successful because they had strong and determined leadership: "We need a lot of people like [that] in our community".

council bureaucracy. Described on its website as 'the biggest and the best' local authority in the UK, Birmingham City Council serves a population of around a million, with a turnover of £2 billion.

Decentralisation developments have appeared uneven. However, in the Aston/Newtown area there appears to be considerable agreement among officers and community representatives that the decentralisation process has been relatively effective, due in part, at least, to the fact that this has built on previous experiences of participation via the City Challenge.

Aston/Newtown has been characterised by high levels of social deprivation and high levels of unemployment (twice the Birmingham average at the time of the City Challenge bid, which was triggered, at least in part, by the closure of one of the last industrial plants in the area). Ethnic minorities have experienced particularly high rates of unemployment.

Key issues identified by regeneration programmes locally have included the quality of housing and other key services (such as street cleaning and environmental services), issues of race and racism, particular issues for Asian women, access to finance and debt problems, community safety, and 'the alternative economy' including drugs. Boundary issues were particularly significant for the City Challenge, defining which communities and streets were included and which excluded from consideration for funding.

In particular, the concentrations of Bengali settlement that were the heart of the Bangladeshi community were largely excluded from City Challenge boundaries. As the result of sustained efforts, by the Bangladeshi community and other stakeholders, these localities were included within the boundaries of the SRB.

Distinctive features

The complexities of race and racism were particularly significant in demonstrating the complexity of 'community' in Aston. Issues of racism and exclusion were important in understanding the tensions of community representation. In addition, the differences of perception and experience within the Bengali community – especially differences relating to age and gender – posed further issues which needed to be addressed within the processes of

"The council is on such a large scale (with some 40,000 employees working for the council). The major departments are huge.... Ward councillors represent wards which are far bigger than elsewhere. Taken together these factors [have] resulted in a representation gap."

"Decentralisation has been working better in Aston/ Newtown as a result of the experiences, knowledge and skills developed through City Challenge and subsequently via the SRB ... and there are now heads of departments who have experience of such local projects."

"LILA is stronger in the City Challenge area precisely because of the experiences of working in City Challenge...."

"... but there is no quick fix for ensuring that community representation is democratically accountable [especially in the complex context of Birmingham]."

representation and resource allocation. There are positive lessons to be learned from experiences of successful challenges to processes of exclusion.

The SRB programme has succeeded in developing good practice in dialogue with local communities, particularly around issues of training and capacity building (building on previous developments of good practice). The SRB has also been described as being closer to local communities, in comparison with City Challenge. But the SRB is also far more modestly resourced, overall, with fewer resources for publicity and logistical support, as a result. This is a limiting factor which inhibits the further development of community participation.

Barnsley, South Yorkshire

Descriptive features

Of the four case study areas, Barnsley has witnessed the most recent and the most extreme form of industrial restructuring. Local employment was historically dominated by the coalmining industry, but this sector collapsed in the 1980s, with particularly marked decline after the 1984/85 coal strike. Between 1984 and 1994 Barnsley lost over 15,000 mining jobs. Total employment in the borough council area fell by 19% between 1981 and 1991 compared to a national decrease of 3% over the same period.

Consequently, the area has been characterised by a wide range of area-based regeneration initiatives and a complex web of partnerships at regional, borough and local levels. Large parts of the area have been eligible for funding under Objective 2 and RECHAR European Commission regimes; two rounds of City Challenge and a range of SRB partnerships have been based locally. In the late 1990s most of the South Yorkshire coalfield, including much of the area of Barnsley Metropolitan Borough Council, was deemed eligible for large-scale funding under the European Objective 1 programme and in 1998 the borough was designated as 'Regeneration Pathfinder' by the Local Government Association under the New Commitment for Regeneration programme.

In the summer/autumn of 1999 the Objective 1 Single Programme Document (SPD) was drafted by the South Yorkshire Forum, a partnership that involves four local authorities (Barnsley, Doncaster, Sheffield and Rotherham), three Training and Enterprise Councils (TECs), local universities, the voluntary sector and the private sector. The Objective 1 Programme is divided between the four themes of education and training, economic restructuring, competitiveness and social exclusion.

The targets that the region has set for itself are high: they include such goals as increasing the number of small businesses in the region by 50% and ensuring that South Yorkshire becomes one of the UK's top regions for ICT skills. Some of the aims from early drafts of the proposals for Objective 1 – such as to increase employment in high technology sectors to 10% above the national

"In Barnsley people always used say that the council do it *for you* and the Coal Board do it *to you*. To a large extent that mentality still prevails."

"The coincidence of economic and political power [in Barnsley] used to be a necessity. Now it is a liability."

"Behind quite a lot of the problems is the malign influence of the Treasury"

"We have a strong sense of community here but we should not forget that most people do not belong to organisations or community groups."

"We have to get away from the notion of seeing young people as part of the problem."

"The best community partnerships have done some fantastic things but the democratic modernisation agenda has set back the community partnerships an awfully long way."

"Around here we are a multi-community community."

"Given the workerist tradition and community solidarity here you have to see why, for some people, a volunteer is somebody who does something for nothing and takes away [other people's] paid work."

average, to decrease average unemployment in the region to the national average and to increase GDP per capita to 90% of the European average by 2010 to 95% by 2010 – might be criticised in some quarters for raising false expectations.

However, approximately £600-£700 million Objective 1 money is scheduled to be spent over seven years in the whole of South Yorkshire (of which Barnsley is only a part). European money will need to be 'match funded' from other sources, clearly a worry locally and a concern of the recently formed government Coalfields Task Force. If matched public sector funding is achieved it should lead to investment of over £1 billion of public sector investment in the region in the next seven years and commensurable sums of private sector investment. However, the fact that the scale of Objective 1 funding for the whole of South Yorkshire came to a smaller figure than the sum invested in the Millennium Dome (situated in another of our case study areas) was also commonly noted.

The SRB 5 programme in Barnsley will focus on capacity building locally to access and prepare for the Objective 1 programme. At the borough level, the Barnsley Development Agency has brought together the economic development sections of both the TEC and the local authority. Voluntary Action Barnsley is a voluntary sector forum for voluntary and community sector representation and serves as the nominating body for most of the local regeneration partnerships.

The council has acted innovatively in recent years to create local community partnerships. These have been established as autonomous companies and attempt to draw together local councillors and community interests.

Also in Barnsley and the surrounding area, there is a concentration of agencies that have attempted to develop 'alternative' forms of economic development through a 'community development trust' model, or other 'community-led' responses to deprivation. In Grimethorpe, at Northern College and at Priory Campus (as well as in the Manor and Castle Development Trust in Sheffield) there are working models of area regeneration that differ significantly from the mainstream conventions of our other case study locations.

Community partnerships in Barnsley

When they work well the community partnerships in Barnsley provide innovative models of 'stakeholder democracy' in action. When first introduced, they were in part rationalised by the greater demands placed on local authorities by Europe to demonstrate community involvement by drawing money down from Rechar 2 and from Objective 2 Priority 5 funds. In their original planning they were intended to create sustainable sites of economic and social change within communities that broke from the local 'statist' conventions. They were designed with the intention of drawing up agendas for regeneration from the 'bottom up' and have been involved with developing bids to the Lottery and other funding bodies. In parts of the area they draw together amenity groups, sports clubs, educational interests and local members to draw up audits and regeneration plans for their areas.

An interesting debate is focused on the degree to which local partnerships challenge or reinforce conventional models of local democracy – particularly in the context of reforms to local government which in Barnsley potentially conflict with the workings of the community partnerships. The introduction of an executive/scrutiny distinction locally has been accompanied by a rearrangement of local authority structures in Barnsley with the 'backbench' members encouraged to fulfil the role of 'community councillors', chairing local forums that operate at a larger scale than the partnerships.

It is fair to note that the successes of the partnerships are not universal. Members of longstanding tenants' and residents' associations expressed unease at the manner in which 'community' was being reinvented in some senses that undermined the conventional and less nuanced solidarities of 'homeplace'. Some councillors were more comfortable than others with the new forms of partnership working that was demanded by their introduction. Effectively the local authority member role changed from one of allocation and decision making to one of facilitation and arbitration.

Distinctive features

The legitimacy of the local authority is subject to far less cynicism in Barnsley than in any of the other case study areas. Political mobilisation has conventionally focused on the Labour Party and the local Labour movement and, consequently, there has been less 'social movement'-based voluntary sector participation. There is also a more dialogic relationship with the Government Regional Office than in some other case study locations.

The scale of economic problems is far greater in Barnsley, as are the resources at stake. It is striking that there has been community representation throughout the Objective 1 process but the degree to which such participation will be able to determine outcomes is yet to be tested.

Barnsley was more homogeneous in terms of both social class and economic base than any of the three other case study areas. This, in part, provides the basis of advantages of trust within communities and the disadvantages associated with both low levels of third sector activity and a very uneven gender balance in many of the regeneration institutions.

The simultaneous existence of both innovative institutions that have developed notions of the social economy and large-scale agencies created to increase inward investment make Barnsley a particularly significant test case. The balance between the call centres that now occupy parts of the old coalfield, the ICT growth envisaged in the Objective 1 Plans and the alternative models of economic development associated with some of the development trust activity locally will provide telling models of the effectiveness and the degree of community participation in area regeneration.

The success of some parts of the borough in establishing alternative models of economic change prompts competition internally for resources. Such a competition is exacerbated by the village-based structure of much of the borough.

Networks in Barnsley have both the strengths of *informality* and *trust* but provide the weaknesses of uneven access to power and resources. The traditionally conceived voluntary sector appears to have deepened its capacity to represent communities of interest in the regeneration process. We also observed strong networks through the Labour Party and the Labour movement that helped channel council thinking about regeneration into the community sector. On the other hand, there are uneven patterns of networking within the loosely defined community sector, weakened by geographical isolation and lack of resources. The increased professionalisation of the voluntary sector promotes its own problems of accountability and representation.

The scarcity of time, the demand for crudely simplified outputs and the local history can lead some decision makers to simplify the complexity of *the community* and consequently to misrepresent its needs.

Acorn Centre, Grimethorpe

In 1983 Barnsley MBC bought the (derelict) site of the Acorn Centre from British Coal. In October 1993 the pit at Grimethorpe closed. The Acorn centre is a member of the Development Trusts Association and has pioneered a range of community-led regeneration initiatives.

Funding:

- originally through Urban Programme, for Phase 1 (the High Street block including the police station);

- through RECHAR 1 for Phase 2 of the building;

- ERDF for businesses, SRB for Acorn management and staff, ESF for training and jobs, FEFC for adult education (Schedule 2);

- BMBC has provided match funding – its biggest capital investment outside of City Challenge.

Its facilities include workspace, meeting rooms, community enterprises, services, business support, adult education and basic skills training. The Acorn has also created its own community-owned call-centre.

The specificity of London

The two London case studies had a number of common features which distinguished them from the Barnsley and Birmingham case studies. While all four areas had suffered from the withdrawal or collapse of key industries, in the two London case study areas, de-industrialisation has been succeeded by new economic interests centred on property development. The escalation of land values in London is often exacerbated by regeneration activity and the strategic locations of both Greenwich and Kings Cross (for Greenwich, proximity to the Thames, the City, Docklands and the Millennium Dome; for Kings Cross, the rail network, including the potential international connections via the proposed Channel Tunnel Rail Link and proximity to central London) have led to further pressures on land values. Private sector interests have had a major role in the politics of regeneration in these areas, and this has limited the potential impact of the community sector, in relation to strategic decisions.

A second, related feature distinguishing the London areas has been the pressure on housing. High property values have resulted in shifts toward luxury private developments, and consequent squeezes on less profitable land uses such as social housing. Third, the extreme complexity of inner London's ethnic composition has resulted in a complicated web of networks and relationships, both positive and negative. Finally, the long histories of regeneration activity in both London areas have resulted in the development of networks of experienced community activists. Positively, this has led to the emergence of a range of community-led initiatives, based on communities' own definitions of their needs. More negatively, these long histories have led to the emergence of considerable cynicism and bitterness, mutual suspicions and fraught partnership situations.

Greenwich Waterfront, South London

Descriptive features

The Greenwich Waterfront stretches along 11km of the Thames in South East London. It encompasses a diverse group of regeneration sites and communities ranging from Thamesmead in the east through Woolwich, the Greenwich peninsular, Greenwich town centre to the area of development around Deptford Creek in the East in partnership with the neighbouring London Borough of Lewisham.

Many of the sites are characterised by large-scale dereliction and contaminated land caused by the disappearance of heavy industrial uses. Unemployment across North Greenwich rose rapidly with the decline of industrial and manufacturing sectors in inner London, particularly in defence-related industries.

Greenwich is an extremely ethnically diverse area. The ethnic minority community is much more mixed than other South Thames boroughs: a third is South Asian (of whom Indians are the largest group); over a third is black African or black Caribbean (with slightly more Caribbeans than Africans); the remaining third includes Chinese, Turkish, Irish and others (Labour Market Assessment, 1993/94). Among the significant small ethnic minority populations are recent refugees from Somalia (concentrated in the East of the borough) and slightly older immigrant communities of Cypriot Turks and ethnic Chinese from Vietnam (concentrated in the West of the borough). There are 34 different first languages spoken in Greenwich schools. Racism is a significant problem in the area; Thamesmead in particular is characterised by 'outer-city racism'. It has been targeted by organised fascism (the British National Party have their national headquarters in nearby Welling) and there have been several racially motivated assaults and murders in the Eastern part of the Waterfront area.

In the mid-1980s, the local authority developed the notion of an overarching 'partnership' structure to serve as an umbrella body that would address the needs of North Greenwich. The Greenwich Waterfront Development Partnership (GWDP), involving private, public and community sectors, came to form the centrepiece of the Greenwich Waterfront Strategy. Subsequently a range of successful bids for SRB funding from central government have been won with delivery agencies established just below the level of the overarching structure. In this way Woolwich Development Agency is delivering a major regeneration programme in Woolwich and Greenwich Development Agency doing likewise in both the Creekside area and the town centre of Greenwich.

The nature of community participation in the regeneration process is consequently at times twofold. At one level the community is 'represented' through an umbrella forum, at another directly on to delivery agencies. The Greenwich Waterfront Community Forum was established in 1992. The Forum coordinates community response and action across the waterfront area and has over 100 affiliated community and voluntary sector groups. Affiliated organisations may nominate delegates to the forum which in turn nominates five members on to the partnership board. At a second level individual delivery agencies some times coordinate alternative mechanisms for community representation. For example the Creekside SRB partnership has a Creekside Community Forum with nominating rights to the SRB Board.

Significantly, Greenwich Waterfront Community Forum (GWCF) was constructed self-consciously in an attempt to provide a form of regeneration that distinguished itself from the Docklands development (which stretches from Wapping to the Royal Docks on the north bank of the river) by the Urban Development Corporation under the London Docklands Development Corporation from 1981 to 1996.

The sheer scale of the exercise in community participation meant that there would never be enough community representatives with the time and energy to cover all the bases effectively. As a result, community input was extremely variable and professionals tended to become drawn into filling the gaps.

Distinctive features

GWDF was in many ways a model of regeneration that was developed precisely to address the exclusion of the local community seen in the London Docklands on the waterfront to the north of Greenwich.

The strengths of the Greenwich structure are most easily summarised by the manner in which the overarching sense of partnership anticipated the direction of urban policy partnership imperatives in the 1990s and has consequently been successful in attracting European and British government funding.

The weaknesses of the structure are the logical corollaries of its strengths: the formal structure of the GWDP is not particularly amenable to complexity, diversity and rapid change in the community sector. Thus, GWCF at times appears to serve as a 'buffer' between the Development Board and community. Both officers of the regeneration agencies and community representatives have suggested that the long-term sustainability of this model is limited to its period of greatest value in the early 1990s.

The forum offers advice on constitutions, where to get funds and other practical issues. As an umbrella organisation it acts as enabler to local groups, assisting their participation in partnership activities. The forum organises public meetings and provides help with photocopying; they also offer childcare support. There is a support worker and an administration budget. They do not offer general help to groups or organisations and do not offer training.

There is inevitably a distance between the structures and spirit of accountability. At times the Greenwich structure was compared unfavourably with the less formal structures in Creekside inherited from the Deptford Community Forum in neighbouring Lewisham. Equally, the informality of the Creekside structure is at times said to promote a 'clique-ishnesss' that Greenwich's formality protects itself from. However, there is a strong middle class presence through amenity groups and in the 'exceptional' nature of Greenwich town centre, and residents' groups that felt under-represented and ethnic minority groups questioned the ability of such formal structures to represent effectively the complexity of community realities.

"The partnership board wants one view [to negotiate with]. It's more convenient for them to 'do business' with a unified view, whilst the reality is that there is a diversity of views."

"It would be helpful if proactive approaches were taken to encourage ethnic minorities to come forward."

"Community involvement affects outcomes very unevenly. Things aren't prioritised by need but by those who've got the loudest mouth, and by networks of grace and favour and scratching backs."

"Community involvement does make an impact on the ways in which the programmes are shaped.... This has gotten better from SRB 1 through to SRB 4 following the development of good practice."

"There's a key difference between community consultation and community participation. Consultation is being asked but having no power. That's not good enough. Too often the consultation is after the decision's been made anyway."

Kings Cross, North London

Descriptive features

The regeneration site of Kings Cross is an area of approximately three square kilometres centred on Kings Cross Railway Station in the London Boroughs of Camden and Islington. It is a strategic site for redevelopment on a major scale, with potentially international dimensions linked to the long-stalled proposal to build the London connection for the Channel Tunnel Rail Link on the site.

The area is characterised by:

- overcrowded housing;
- high levels of homeless people and rough sleepers;
- over 23 hectares of derelict land around the railways;
- a disproportionate number of single-person households and single-parent households compared to London averages;
- diverse minority ethnic populations – the largest being the Bangladeshi, Irish and Black African communities;
- high levels of deprivation and racial tension;
- large number of young people – 32% of the area's population is aged under 18;
- extensive drug and alcohol abuse;
- a prominent sex industry;
- poor-quality street environments.

An SRB award of £37.5 million for a seven-year programme was made to the Kings Cross Partnership (KCP) by the Government Office for London in December 1995. Combined with other public and private sector investment the total KCP programme is £251 million. KCP's vision for the area is for it to be transformed into a new quarter for London, which is:

- an important and successful part of a world city;
- a major interchange for travel information and culture;
- a destination in its own right for a wide range of activities;
- a safe and pleasant place to live and work in, to travel through and visit;
- a high-quality environment with an accessible and integrated mix of uses;
- a tolerant multi-racial community with excellent employment opportunities.

"Drug users, drinkers, people hanging around in the street, asylum seekers – they are not seen to be part of the community."

"The leaders and councillors at board meetings need KCP to work. The council regeneration departments need for it to be a success, so the learning from mistakes and integrating them into local political decision making and mainstream service provision doesn't happen because they are all stakeholders in these projects and need to see good outputs."

"I think that there is a feeling that the money is on one side and you are on the other."

"We have the paradoxical situation that Kings Cross is awash with money; there has never been so much money in the area – build anything you like – but there isn't the money to run a service."

"It is not perfect, but are you going to get anything better? But it's all going to take time – you cannot get democracy off the shelf, like a soap powder."

"The whole system of partnership is bureaucratic – worse than the local authority."

The KCP has a board of representatives including six from private companies (including major landowners), six community representatives (two council leaders and four community representatives), two representatives from each local authority area in Camden and six from a number of statutory agencies and social landlords. KCP also runs a number of consultative fora: the Social and Community Forum, the Economic Forum and the St Pancras Forum. The work of KCP is scrutinised in the Monitoring and Project Approval committees which involve KCP staff and board members, and working groups of a range of organisations have met to consider issues relevant to young people, homelessness, health and sport and leisure at different points of the programme.

Some of these structures arose from joint community, local authority and statutory agencies' past initiatives on crime, drug abuse and prostitution. In 1992 the Kings Cross Joint Working Party was established to provide a forum for local debate and agree strategy; this formed the basis for membership of the Kings Cross Partnership Community Forum.

In March 1997 the Kings Cross Community Development Project was established with SRB support. The project allocates the Community Chest of KCP on an annual basis and commissioned a study by the Community Development Foundation, which formed the basis for the 1998 Community Development Strategy for the Kings Cross area. The project is now establishing itself as an independent organisation "to strengthen the community and voluntary sector contribution to the sustainable regeneration of Kings Cross" and is seeking to acquire and refurbish a building in the area for both project activities and as a source of revenue funds.

Local participation structures also exist in part of the KCP area. Both London boroughs have local advisory fora which provide a means for selecting and holding to account community representatives for the KCP Board – although not all of them. This lack of consistency on the selection of the community representatives was a key problem for some participants at the start of the KCP programme. There is also some controversy in the history of some local partnership structures in the Kings Cross area: the Somerstown Area Partnership collapsed in 1997 amid disputes with the London Borough of Camden, and some working groups of the St Pancras Forum were convened to consider land development issues over a period and then ceased operating amid confusion and bad feeling.

A number of other area-based initiatives also operate within each of the local authorities involved in the KCP – West Euston SRB, a Health Action Zone and a Housing Capital Challenge.

Both boroughs have umbrella voluntary sector organisations and a range of community and voluntary sector organisations are active, although the local authority boundaries are a significant factor in the overall availability and provision of services in the KCP area.

Overall, Kings Cross has a long and successful history of community activity over past decades – in particular, the local umbrella group, the Kings Cross Railway Lands Group, has brought community organisations together across the two constituent boroughs to address strategic planning issues. This history of community organisation has been a key factor, contributing to the strength of local interest and the extent of local expertise in relation to strategic issues.

Distinctive features

The context for the work of the Kings Cross Partnership is dominated by the major uncertainty surrounding the planning and approval of the Channel Tunnel Rail Link. Its impact in terms of planning blight on local property and the future development of the 'Railway Lands' – the largest inner-city brownfield site in Europe – is the subject of keen local debate involving major land and property owners. Key issues for participants in regeneration are the tension between large-scale property development targeted at maximising the commercial value of the land and benefiting visitors and transport users, against the needs of existing highly-deprived resident communities for jobs, affordable housing, safe play areas and so on.

The function of Kings Cross as a major transport hub also means that the area is the arrival point for refugees and asylum seekers, as well as the homeless and roofless. Recent legislative changes have increased the numbers of people experiencing problems with temporary accommodation, homelessness and associated vulnerability to crime.

In addition to these uncertainties the KCP
underwent major internal change over the period
of the study. In its early years senior executives
responsible for the overall programme and
coordination of community input changed and the
formal responsibilities for delivery of the
programme were sub-contracted to Stratford
Development Partnership – an independent not-
for-profit regeneration agency.

As with other case study areas a good deal of
instability in the community and voluntary sector
driven by the availability of financial resources,
created some tensions over allocation of various
parts of the KCP programme for participants.
During the period of this study, mainstream cuts
in support of these organisations, particularly in
the London Borough of Islington, had a major
impact on participants' perceptions of the
programme and who it was seen to benefit.

The partnership also straddles two local authority
areas, with different procedures and operational
requirements for decision making both on policy
and practical projects. The London Borough of
Islington is the formal accountable body for SRB
funds but dealing with this division in
responsibility for a relatively small regeneration
area is a distinctive feature of Kings Cross as a
case study.

Summary of findings

This chapter summarises the main findings from the research. The findings are set out in the order in which the original research questions were framed: What were the views of local participants – community representatives, community activists and the professionals who worked with them – on the following questions?

1. How do participants evaluate the lessons of their experiences of participation in area regeneration programmes, for building integrated, sustainable, democratically accountable structures for community participation? (This question has been divided into two parts: representation/accountability and sustainability.)
2. How do participants evaluate the technical and professional support which was available to them, to facilitate their participation in area regeneration programmes?
3. How do participants evaluate their impact, through participating in area regeneration programmes, including monitoring and evaluation?

As the previous section has already pointed out, participants had generally had few – if indeed any – opportunities for reflecting on the lessons of their experiences, either individually or collectively. This was true for officers as well as for community representatives and activists. When opportunities were offered, participants responded overwhelmingly positively, actively engaging with the research process. A number of participants commented on this, expressing the view that there needed to be more opportunities for reflection, to share learning, both within area regeneration programmes and across programmes. Despite the pressures on people's time, significant numbers did participate in monitoring and evaluation, and in developing

effective tools for auditing community participation. The research team benefited greatly from participants' support and from their generosity with their time – which was particularly appreciated – given how very busy so many of the participants were.

Through the responses to the research questions, a number of overall themes emerged, themes that have already been outlined in the previous section. In particular, the diversity and continuing processes of change were striking, as were the differences between the four areas and the differences of community interests within them. This diversity made it all the more relevant to question the mechanisms for representation and accountability; who was effectively representing whom and how did this representation relate to wider questions about democratic accountability and processes of social exclusion? The conflicting pressures on community representatives emerged, along with the promotion of 'community stars', together with the pressures on the community sector more generally, and its potential professionalisation. This made the case for more systematic provision of appropriate resourcing and independent support for the community sector all the more compelling.

Through the research process, and particularly through the final workshops, which brought participants from the four case study areas together, participants shared local experiences and reflected on wider policy concerns. They raised a number of issues about area regeneration policies and practice, exploring the need for changes at regional and national level as well as locally. They also raised questions about the interface between small area policies and mainstream policies more generally. The concluding section returns to some of the implications for participation, at both regional and national levels.

The findings

How do participants evaluate the lessons of their experiences of participation in area regeneration programmes, for building integrated, sustainable, democratically accountable structures for community participation?

Is community participation being developed in ways which are representative and democratically accountable?

There have been examples of good practice and these have been illustrated through the four case study profiles in Chapter 2. Community participation structures and processes have been developed as lessons have been learnt from one area regeneration programme to another. Overall, later SRB programmes, building on new guidelines, have offered improved opportunities for community participation.

However, the research also identified a number of issues, which present continuing problems. There is evidence from the four case studies which indicates that community representation – both on partnership boards and via community participation forums – has been problematic in previous area regeneration programmes. There are continuing issues which need to be addressed.

Had agendas been set before effective community participation structures were set in place?

Agendas and targets had already been established as part of the bidding process, in programmes in each of the four case study areas. The board's focus was then targeted on these (official) agendas, leaving insufficient space for community-based agendas, as these have emerged.

As one community representative put it, the community felt "saddled with 'outputs' which exclude community concerns".

While these were continuing issues, it should be emphasised that improvements in subsequent regeneration programmes were both recognised and welcomed. The notion of the Year Zero (a preliminary year for planning and consultation, prior to implementation) – to enable fuller consultation and negotiation to take place *before* programmes were fully operationalised – was generally seen as offering a significant move forward.

Recognising diversity within communities

Community representatives were expected to represent 'the community view', but the reality is that communities are rarely homogeneous: there are often conflicting interest and perspectives. For example, there may be tensions between the people who live in an area and the people who work there; there may be tensions between voluntary and community sector workers who have worked in a particular community for many years and those who believe themselves 'authentic' members of the community because they live in a particular place (the tension between the 'wage slip' and the 'rent book' definitions of the local community). Such tensions may become obstacles to successful area regeneration, although both residents and workers in a locality have a legitimate contribution to make to the area's well-being. Other potential sources of tension about who is, and who is not, effectively defined as being included in 'the community' emerged in relation to questions of ethnicity, gender, sexuality, age, class and housing tenure (with particular debates around whether or not homeless people were considered a part of the 'community').

If diversity and differences are not fully recognised and taken into account, many voices are not effectively heard; this applies especially to black and ethnic minority voices in areas with ethnic minority communities (three of the four case study areas). Under-representation emerged as an issue in each of these areas. In South East London, for example, there was a widely held view that black and Asian groups had been effectively excluded. Black community professionals perceived the council as reluctant to fund black groups (which meant that they were less likely to be provided with professional support to engage with SRB structures), black groups commented on their difficulties in gaining access to information, with consequent difficulties in gaining access to resources: "We're trying to catch up all the time ... we get left the crumbs".

Even when efforts were made, they were not necessarily effective – expecting one black person to represent the diversity of black and ethnic minority views in an area could be seen as tokenism: one community representative commented, "I was the only black face on the board and there was a kind of tokenism".

There were also cases where the effective exclusion of black and ethnic minority communities had been successfully challenged. In Aston/Newtown, Birmingham, for example, the Bangladeshi Youth Forum (BYF) had succeeded in overcoming their original exclusion from City Challenge, and BYF are now partners in the voluntary and community sector-led SRB in the area.

Working class voices were also under-represented in mixed class areas (a factor which was particularly relevant in the two London case study areas): a community activist in South East London remarked that, "They call it a community but it isn't", and went on to cite a case where middle-class community representatives had opposed a particular development proposal despite the fact that it had been supported by most of the working-class people who actually lived in the area in question. These conflicts of interest were particularly significant in areas such as Kings Cross, and around the Millennium site in Greenwich, where there were such major development issues at stake. There were also criticisms of situations in which "workers (that is, professional workers) were there representing members of the community" rather than enabling community members to speak for themselves (this particular comment referred to experiences of participation structures in Kings Cross).

Other groups which emerged as being under-represented included homeless people (although despite the contentious nature of this issue, there were also successful attempts to involve homeless people in Kings Cross), refugees, people with physical and/or mental disabilities, and lesbians and gay men. Young people were under-represented in each of the case study areas although there were also particular instances where attempts to involve young people had been more effective. For example, outreach youth work had been more successful than attempting to persuade young people to attend formal meetings in Kings Cross, and young people had been involved through schools in Birmingham, using video. In Greenwich the development of a young people's council has actively sought to involve young people in

democratic processes and in neighbouring Lewisham there has been an ambitious programme to involve young people, including a programme of outreach youth work. But these were the exceptions rather than the norm:

> "There's a culture of not valuing women and young people. This is about the unconscious cultural norms of the older men." (Council officer in Barnsley)

Good practice: The homelessness sub-group of Kings Cross Partnership

Some SRB activity helped to create transitional structures that allowed existing groups to both access SRB funds and focus discussions with mainstream service providers. In Kings Cross a homelessness worker from a local voluntary organisation convened a regular focus group on homelessness which secured research funds from the partnership to map local needs and develop a set of principles for housing strategies in the Kings Cross area. As a result of this work KCP also funded 'Speakouts' for local homeless people to speak to local government decision makers from social services and housing departments, and resulted in changes to local authority housing department procedures for people in Bed & Breakfast accommodation. This raises further questions about follow-up and the extent to which housing and homelessness issues are being addressed at the policy level.

Competing pressures on community representatives: the making – and breaking – of 'community stars'

Becoming a community representative led to mixed benefits and often to very stressful experiences. A number of community representatives felt that they were being squeezed between community expectations, on the one hand, and, in practice, not being listened to on the board, on the other. This view was shared by community professionals working with them: "Stuck in the middle", as one community professional put this. If community representatives became too close to officials on the board, they could become detached from the communities they represented:

"They can become seen by other parts of the community as part of the problem rather than as part of the solution." (Senior officer who had identified this as a problem in his area)

But community representatives could, conversely, also be dismissed as being 'unrepresentative' when the board or council did not want to hear what they were saying. One community activist commented that the council (seen as the key player in the area, also with private sector interests) wanted representatives who were "solid establishment figures; people who will not under any circumstances rock the boat". A community professional from the same area agreed: "They prefer 'yes' people".

Similar tensions existed in another area, where there were comparable pressures on community representatives:

"The local establishment see professionalisation as a good thing; they like to see individuals becoming effectively full-time unpaid community professionals. This is ideological rhetoric; there should be more of a role for occasional whingers. It's a question of how people can engage without giving up too much regular time. One reason why the senior officers and members like to see the development of individual community reps into community professionals is so they can develop one-to-one relationships, so they have a single person to go to when they want to negotiate with a community. For lower officers, it's more about ... developing local people who can speak their language." (Council officer)

"There is lots of pressure on individuals once they get identified as spokespeople" (Community activists)

These tensions were recognised both by the community representatives themselves and the professionals who were working with them – "less than credible" was how one community professional described the position of community representatives. As a professional (from another case study area) put it, "some of our 'stars' of community participation become victims" and

suffer considerable personal stress, because of these conflicting pressures.

Participation is very time-consuming

As well as being very stressful for 'community stars' who become deeply involved as community representatives, participation is very time-consuming – too many meetings to attend, too many papers to digest – and this was generally agreed to be a major problem. The contribution of unpaid community representatives needs to be more effectively recognised and valued. Several community representatives did go on to comment that they had personally developed strategies to cope – learning to say 'no' to yet more demands on their time.

Lack of 'transparency'

A lack of transparency emerged as a particular problem in some cases. For example, if board papers were not publicly available, community representatives were placed in difficult positions about reporting back. The whole participation process often took place with such speed that there was little time for feedback, and not much official pressure for feedback to take place anyway. Despite these pressures, there were also comments of appreciation about those community representatives who did succeed in reporting back effectively to the communities they were representing.

Lack of independent support and technical back-up

The patchy provision of independent support and technical back up for community representatives was identified as a significant problem. For example, community representatives complained about being asked to comment on papers, without having had any prior briefing on the issues involved. This problem also applied, to some extent, in voluntary or community-based boards, which also generated pressures on their representatives. As one board member on a voluntary/community sector-led SRB commented, the SRB actually had fewer resources for this type of back-up, in comparison with the much larger (and better resourced) City Challenge which had preceded the SRB.

Some black groups (in South East London) specifically commented that they had not had the benefit of community work support and argued that community workers concentrated on working with well-established groups which were disproportionately white. As a result, black and ethnic minority groups were disadvantaged. One community representative commented that "black and ethnic minority groups do not know that the board is giving money", let alone know how to access these resources.

Nevertheless, as the following section illustrates, there were also instances where community representatives and community activists had been

Local resources in Barnsley

In the Barnsley case study area, many participants emphasised the positive role played by centres such as Priory Campus and the Acorn (Grimethorpe) (see p 14). Some of these centres had been created in previous area regeneration programmes and others are provided by the community services section of the local council in villages in the borough. People felt that they were a useful focus of support to community activity, and benefited from their multi-purpose uses, including cafés, training rooms and provision of local health, advice and training by statutory and voluntary sector agencies.

effectively supported, and received appropriate training (to meet their learning needs as they defined them). Where appropriate support had been available, this had been very much valued.

Specific issues in relation to community forum-type structures

There were specific comments about particular problems that arose in community forum-type participation structures. One of the key underlying problems was that these forums were typically set up on the assumption that the community was homogenous. The community forum would therefore be expected to represent 'the community view'. As it has already been suggested, the reality is more complex and more problematic.

In addition, there were particular problems and expressions of dissatisfaction when there was:

- inadequate notice of meetings;
- inadequate minutes;
- confusion about what decisions had been made (including lack of information about spending procedures and decisions).

Finally, there were criticisms about the limited remit of community participation forums, in two of the four areas. Community representation was "stereotypically consigned to the 'community chest' level of vision and practice". In other words communities were being encouraged to focus on the allocation of small grants, rather than on the wider strategic policy issues. This was particularly problematic in London, where the strategic issues involved major and potentially competing interests. As a community representative (from another London area) commented, there has been a view (attributed to the local council) that "you should be concentrating your efforts on the little things and be satisfied with tiny grants". This exacerbated competition between different groups in the voluntary and community sector "vying for the support of official circles".

"There are issues of the pepperpot funding areas, which lead to problems over economies of scale, especially for small organisations. There are related issues over jealousies from communities on the peripheries of areas designated as falling within the funding regimes. These factors can dis-unite communities from each other, and lead to fault-lines within the community partnership area". (Council officer)

"For some people, there was very real competition for resources between areas. There was resentment at the way [poorer areas] got everything, although other people felt that clearly places like that needed more resources. Resentment focused on the way areas considered to be richer (eg areas described as 'two-car' areas) got less." (Community partnership focus group in the same area)

However, it was also pointed out that:

"It's much easier to make an argument for resources for levelling up, and much harder to make an argument that without resources there'll be levelling down." (Community partnership focus group)

Other people in this group took what they saw as the 'broader picture' and understood why some places got more resources than others. They pointed out that, "We just have to be cleverer in making our demands". It was also pointed out that these sorts of arguments are not new: it was the same when it was purely the council allocating resources.

There were a number of more general comments about area regeneration programmes and the increasing competition and conflicts between organisations and groups in the voluntary and community sectors. These comments have wider implications for small area programmes more generally, and for their relationship – or lack of relationship – to mainstream policies. Chapter 4 returns to these questions, and the importance of addressing the broader implications of participation and developing processes of dialogue, bottom-up as well as top-down.

Participation structures

> Are community participation structures likely to survive beyond the life of the regeneration programme?

Overall, comments on the likely sustainability of community forum-type structures were negative in two of the four areas. Experiences had clearly been negative, especially in the early days of City Challenge in Birmingham and in the first phase in Kings Cross.

"Can't see any basis for continuity." (Community activist)

"I don't think it will last; nor should either." (Community professional in the same area)

These views were not unanimously held and others made more positive comments. There was some recognition that community participation structures were needed on a continuing basis, however, and such structures needed ongoing resourcing.

In Birmingham, in particular, it emerged that, even if community forum structures were unlikely to survive, other structures to facilitate community participation had actually been strengthened. For example some Housing Liaison Boards and decentralisation structures such as 'Local Involvement Local Action' were working more effectively, because of the knowledge, skills and experience gained through City Challenge and SRB. Both community representatives and the professionals who worked with them commented on these achievements (and this view was shared by senior officers).

There were also comments about the links – or lack of links – between community participation structures and local political structures for democratic representation, and the likely sustainability of these links. Although there were positive comments in the context of decentralisation initiatives in Birmingham, there were a number of negative comments. Local councillors were criticised if they were seen as being unsupportive and/or were seen to be trying to exercise control over the community sector. Criticisms of this type were also made in both the London case study areas and Barnsley to a lesser extent.

In Barnsley, it was felt that the community partnerships had been moving towards sustainability, but that the introduction of a parallel system of area forums (as part of the council's implementation of modernising local government) presented new challenges as well as new opportunities.

Sustainability and the community sector more generally

While there was some considerable scepticism about the likely sustainability of community forum-type structures, there were far more positive comments about the likely sustainability of other community-based structures. People spoke with enthusiasm and commitment about the likely sustainability of their own organisations (such as their local tenants' and residents' associations, their community youth organisations and their local umbrella organisations and networks), and people commented about their increasing involvement more generally. An officer in Birmingham commented that, "Rather than being out on a limb, people are linked into decision making structures". This view was widely shared among both professionals and community representatives and activists, who commented on how local people had learnt how to make more impact: "People have become very wise very quickly" (Local authority officer).

There were also comments about the developing strength of the community sector, overall, building on experiences of coping with earlier programmes. In one area, for example, an umbrella group noted their increased ability to share experiences and to work together collaboratively.

In another area, there were comments on the progress that had been made in developing community-based initiatives for regeneration; this was despite the earlier comments about increasing competition between organisations and groups. One view was that the arrival of SRB funds had pushed local groups into working on their proposals together.

> "To give them credit ... it forced people to work together more.... The SRB meant that there was more pressure to set up ... the whole point of SRB is that if you don't work in partnership you don't get the money...." (Community professional/ voluntary sector worker)

Overall, however, the question of sustainability raised related questions about the likely availability of continuing resources: "What about continuing resources to support these [participation structures]?" After City Challenge finished, a community activist remarked that a number of projects "fell because there was no backing". Would this happen to other initiatives?

> "Even a big organisation [like the local voluntary service council] is going to find it difficult to survive." (Professional from another area)

The overall impact on the voluntary/community sector

A number of community activists, community representatives and community professionals raised their wider concerns about the potential incorporation of the community sector. These concerns also emerged in focus group discussions.

Sustainability and development trusts

The sustainability strategy for area-based programmes in two cases study areas has been the creation of a development trust to run building assets created by the programmes. The legacy of a previous City Challenge programme in Barnsley – Priory Campus – is a development trust which uses the building asset created by City Challenge to provide for community needs through service provision by tenants of the centre and by using the rents from other building occupants and uses.

In another case, a community development trust will be created from community development projects funded by the SRB partnership: a building asset is still being identified for a similar arrangement to those at Priory Campus. (SEU, 1999b, Chapter 5, stresses the importance of social enterprise in area regeneration in terms of intermediate labour markets, skills and employment. Our report echoes the particular finding about the significance of sustainable intermediate organisations in processes of area regeneration and reinforces SEU's recommendations about the need to recognise the significance of social enterprise in SRB guidelines and in the work of the Regional Development Agencies and the Small Business Service.)

There were comments about the pressures to focus on and respond to official agendas even when these distracted groups' or organisations' attention away from their own community agendas. This emerged as a particular problem in areas where councils have strong (paternalistic) views about the voluntary and community sector, and about which groups are, or are not, 'acceptable'. Groups felt that they were being defined as 'acceptable' in terms of how far their agendas coincided with council agendas or with private sector interests (such as property development interests). Black and ethnic minority groups were particularly concerned about this problem – maintaining a much-needed service to excluded sections of the community was seen to be more important than trying to fit into council agendas for regeneration. They commented on how they felt that they were constantly having to "bend to suit [funding] requirements", to the detriment of their own community needs and agendas.

There were also more general concerns expressed about the restructuring of the community sector. With increasing professionalisation some groups and organisations were seen as becoming more skilled in obtaining resources. Meanwhile, other groups (especially groups without paid staff, including a disproportionate number of small black groups) were losing out altogether. The professionalisation of the community sector was also seen as leading to exclusion along class lines, as the skills and technologies required for professionalisation are not evenly distributed. As one community professional commented, community groups needed, as a minimum requirement, access to independent technical and professional advice and support on a continuing basis.

In addition, there were related concerns about the overall impact on the community sector: were these processes of change leading to a weakening of the community sector's independent voice? And there were increasing conflicts between groups and areas when they found themselves competing for scarce resources.

Although these wider concerns are important, they do need to be set in the context of the positive aspects which were also identified.

- The community sector was actually developing in strength, through its experiences of participation.
- Both individuals and groups had learnt key lessons about how to work more effectively within regeneration structures. Conversely, it was also suggested that community organisations could have been strengthened in other ways, without having to "jump on the treadmill" of regeneration funding processes:

  "There are better ways of doing that....
  A lot of what you have to learn is
  redundant outside this rather esoteric
  world of regeneration funding".
  (Community professional)

- Some groups had succeeded in combating their original exclusion (there were examples of this in two of the case study areas).
- Alliances and solidarity had developed as groups and organisations had collaborated in response to the opportunities and challenges posed by area regeneration programmes.

Technical and professional support

How do participants evaluate the technical and professional support which was available to them, to facilitate their participation in area regeneration programmes?

Overall, responses to these questions have been mixed. This is consistent with the national picture, which has been described as 'patchy' to say the least (Henderson and Mayo, 1998).

Positive comments

There were a number of positive comments indicating how much technical support, community work support and training has actually been valued, when this has been provided in relevant and accessible ways. Independent professional and technical advice had been important, especially in areas such as Kings Cross where there were complex planning issues involved.

Particular back-up services have been valued (administrative support, assistance with form-filling and access to word-processing facilities were mentioned as examples of useful back-up services). Community representatives in one area especially commented that such support had been provided, and that this had been in an office which was seen as welcoming and friendly to local people.

Particular individuals were valued, including particular officers as well as particular community development workers – those "gatekeepers who want to help you through the gate rather than keep you out". Particular training events have also been useful (such as 'away-days' for board representatives).

Overall there was evidence of some excellent practice. There have been cases where community organisations have been access to continuing community work and training support – which has been negotiated with the organisations in question, to meet their learning needs as they have defined these, themselves. For instance, community representatives in Birmingham referred to training events that had been negotiated to meet their training needs. These ranged from very practical sessions on computing skills or housing maintenance issues, through to broader questions such as how to build democratic organisational structures and practices, how to challenge racism and how to promote empowerment. For example, at one such away-day, a community representative reflected, they had "looked at where we're at and where we want to go ... projected our aim, our goals for next year". Another community representative referred to the value of his experiences, attending a European-level event, where he had enjoyed opportunities "to share experiences", and to address issues of empowerment and democracy. Those who had visited projects in other areas to share ideas, similarly commented on how valuable these exchanges had been. Several people commented on the contrast between traditional forms of training and these negotiated learning opportunities. The contributions of several individuals (locally well known and trusted) community educators and community development workers emerged as a significant factor in achieving these positive outcomes.

A number of those who had valued learning experiences also commented on the importance of the overall atmosphere – 'friendly' and 'relaxed' were terms that were used in this context. "Vital but relaxed. We enjoy it when we go", reflected another community representative, referring to regular away-day sessions as "really good".

There were also a number of comments about the importance of practical aspects of the organisation of training. Childcare was referred to in this context, as key to success – especially for residential sessions: participants appreciated having the time and space to focus on their learning, without domestic hassles.

More generally, both individuals and groups commented on how much they learnt through their experiences of participation, and on the knowledge, skills and confidence they had developed as a result.

Residents Association Information Link (RAIL)

RAIL is a forum through which community organisations and tenants' and residents' groups in Aston/Newtown, Birmingham, come together to share experiences and develop joint action around issues of common concern: "RAIL is about informing each other and developing solidarity". RAIL was formed "to help people feel able to participate fully" including providing support with specific knowledge and skills, enabling people "to have the confidence to take responsibility for managing money, running projects" for instance. RAIL is run by its members, who plan their meetings and workshops, together with the community worker who works with them as a facilitator.

RAIL organises training, where this is relevant, to meet community training needs as local groups define them: "We control the agenda". Training sessions have been organised on a range of relevant topics and issues around regeneration and service delivery, to meet the information needs of RAIL, as identified by RAIL members: "If we've wanted to know something about housing or CCT we'd invite somebody up to explain". Community professionals have suggested that, given the interest shown by community organisations in other areas, the RAIL concept could usefully be developed and applied in other parts of the city.

More negative comments

While it is important to celebrate good practice, the reality is that such good practice seems to have been patchy, to say the least. There was evidence of key gaps in the provision of essential support and back-up services. This included key gaps in support for board representatives: one of the community representatives on an SRB board reflected that she had asked for training when she was elected, but did not receive it. "There's been very little training", concluded one of the London community representatives, going on to highlight the need for more expert advice on technical issues if community representatives are to be in a position to question proposals effectively.

There were criticisms of the lack of resources available for publicity for effective consultation. This was identified as a structural problem, rather than a specific problem in one area – the 5%

budget for management and administration in SRB programmes was criticised for being insufficient, for these purposes.

There were particular criticisms of the lack of support for community groups who were working up their own projects (for example, one community group that asked for assistance were simply told to go away and write a business plan on their own, without professional or financial advice).

There were experiences of inappropriate training (for example, trainers being 'parachuted in' from outside and/or training not being targeted to local needs).

There were particular criticisms about the misuse of consultants, who were "paid considerable sums to tell people what they knew already" (whether this was information held in other local agencies or within communities). As one community professional commented, "The council will look to outside consultants before it looks to its own experts within its own borough". Local organisations and groups could be supported to tender bids to do some of this type of action research work, building on local knowledge and skills. It was also suggested that, where consultants are used, local representatives should be invited to participate on the steering committees which oversee their work.

In addition it was proposed that communities needed a glossary, which explained professional jargon.

It was also notable that both professionals and community activists raised similar points about these issues, with considerable recognition that professionals also need training if they are being asked to work in new ways.

These points about the need for training and other ongoing resources for the community sector applied, more generally, beyond the confines of particular area regeneration programmes. But again participants pointed to contradictions in policy and practice. As participants in a community partnership focus group in Barnsley commented:

> "There is a contradiction when the council and its leader talk up the cabinet-style approach and a listening council while they're taking away a community partnership's support worker, taking away

precisely that which had enabled and held expertise."

Monitoring and evaluating community impact

How do participants evaluate their impact, through participating in area regeneration programmes, including monitoring and evaluation?

There were a number of positive comments about the impact of community participation which can be characterised as follows.

There were examples of local initiatives and projects where community views had been considered in ways which were seen as satisfactory by those concerned. For example, the consultation process over the planning and development of the St George's Centre in Birmingham was described as "a nice story about community involvement, because it has worked". This view was endorsed by a number of community representatives, who valued the services that were to be provided at the centre, once it was operational (such as adult education classes, including recreational classes at reasonable cost).

One community professional commented more generally that "good things do happen". A community representative in another area commented, "We do have some influence on the board", and continued to provide examples of groups, such as refugees and homeless children, whose needs had been placed on the agenda by community representatives on the board. Generally, however, comments of this type related to specific initiatives (such as housing estate improvements, security systems, street lighting, street cleaning and rubbish collection together with projects funded via community chest-type mechanisms).

Overall, a number of community representatives and professionals commented that there was significantly more scope for community participation now, as compared with previous regeneration programmes (such as City Challenge and the first rounds of SRB).

> "There is now more focus upon capacity building ... processes are more effectively

managed.... People in deprived areas are getting empowered – becoming more effective in challenging." (Senior officer)

A community representative expressed a similar view when he reflected that City Challenge had been "horrendous" whereas now, he felt that, "they have started to listen and started to rectify some of the mistakes they made". Similarly a community professional in another area commented that there was now more community involvement – and at an earlier stage:

> "This has gotten better from SRB 1 through to SRB 4."

> "We gained respect and that has given us power." (Community representative in another area)

The situation continues to be dynamic. Even in areas where community activists had felt most marginalised and ignored, changes of key personnel had clearly raised aspirations for improved communication in future.

> "She [a former chief officer in KCP] did nothing in that direction [community participation]. Since [the new chief officer] has brought it forward the officers work as hard as they can." (Resident activist and businessman)

More negative comments

While it is important to recognise and to value positive achievements and developments, a range of more negative comments also need to be taken into account.

Community views tended to be heard only – or at least mainly – when these coincided with official or private sector views, or when they related to relatively peripheral decisions.

> "People had most say on the smaller projects." (Officer)

> "But nothing on the big issues." (Community representative from the same area)

Community representatives referred to feelings of disappointment about progress in relation to the big issues like employment: "Too few people [are] benefiting from jobs which had been coming into the area and unemployment is still high". More generally, there were a number of sceptical comments about community consultation exercises which were seen as being carried out "so that the board can say, 'We consulted', more of a public [relations] exercise".

> "The agendas are set by the council who have pre-agenda meetings." (Community representative from another area)

Where there have been significant conflicts of interest, community views have been marginalised or not heard at all – even excluded deliberately, it has been argued. Such views have been expressed both by community representatives and by community professionals and senior officers. Conflicts of interest of this type have been a particular issue where there have been competing perspectives on strategic land use planning decisions. As one community representative commented, even the partnership board "can't do anything about the [...] land; it is owned by two major companies" – these companies were not prepared to do anything until the outcome of a particular development proposal was finalised. In this area, a number of community representatives argued that they had been deliberately kept away from particular meetings (at the initial phase), for fear that their presence (and their arguments) might offend the private sector interests in question.

Monitoring and evaluation systems were criticised for concentrating on very specific outputs with very little focus on processes. Overemphasising the achievement of particular outputs, such as particular spending targets, can actually lead to the inefficient use of resources – a point which was illustrated with specific examples. Monitoring and evaluation processes were insufficiently transparent, in any case, and there were pressures on all stakeholders to present positive results. The culture of area regeneration programmes was still focused on achieving targets, with little space for risk-taking so that programmes could be genuinely innovative. Other participants, for instance in South East London, criticised the artificial divide between 'outputs' (which are 'monitored') and 'impacts' (which are 'evaluated'), and the emphasis on the former.

In particular, there was little, if any, emphasis on

monitoring the impact of regeneration processes on the strength and independence of the community sector, community capacity building and the development of 'social capital'. This was despite the fact that more recent programmes did include these aspects (that is, capacity building and the development of social capital) as overall aims.

The research team has been particularly struck by these omissions, and by the lack of safe space for critical reflection, because there was so much potential interest in learning from experiences of community participation in area regeneration programmes. Both officers and community activists referred to the extent of their learning, as a result of their participation. In the words of one officer "[Officers] had their eyes opened to new ways of working". Community representatives made similar comments, both about officers' learning and about the extent of their own learning from the process of being involved: "People have learnt a lot over the years ... the officers have learnt too" (Community representative). "People are so much more aware of how things work", commented another representative, and so much more confident in challenging, if they are not satisfied. Through the research process, both in individual interviews and particularly in group discussions, many participants commented on the value of reflecting on their experiences and exchanging views. Participative monitoring and evaluation systems would enable these lessons to be shared and fed back more systematically, both locally and beyond. There was some evidence that, as a result of these learning gains, community organisations were building alliances more effectively.

But, there was scope for extending these processes. Another officer felt that, despite all the learning that had taken place in and between communities, there were still problems about how the lessons were being learned within local authority structures: "[This learning] is not necessarily being conveyed more widely in the rest of the authority". This, in turn, raises questions about how effectively local authorities work across departmental boundaries, in any case.

Key policy and spending issues with major regional and/or national implications have not featured on the agenda. For example, key issues about the structure of regeneration programmes

themselves (including questions about the inherent problems associated with small area initiatives) have not been up for discussion. In particular, small areas which border on city centres or key development sites cannot be regenerated in isolation, without taking account of the wider impact. Physical improvements in such areas can lead to increased land and rental values and the consequent displacement of low-income residents who are unable to compete against more profitable land uses. Critics have pointed to the lack of opportunities for community representatives to put these questions onto the regeneration agenda.

Nor has there been sufficient space to address questions about the extent to which special programmes divert resources from main spending programmes or attempt to compensate for reductions in main spending programmes. This does not mean that community representatives had no views to express on these topics however. On the contrary, both community representatives and the professionals who worked with them did raise such questions. For example, questions were raised about housing policy overall, and more specifically about the lack of affordable housing: "There seems to be a consensus that the quantity of housing is no longer an issue – that only improvements of existing housing is needed" (Community representative). This representative went on to point to the number of people she knew who "cannot get permanent housing because there is none, but that's not an issue for some reason". "Housing", she concluded, "is off the agenda".

This last point relates to the final criticism: that there have not been effective channels for communicating community views directly to government at regional and national levels. For example, both professionals (including senior officers) and community activists remarked that national housing policies currently reinforce the ways in which people with multiple problems become concentrated within particular geographical areas and housing estates. Community representatives and the professionals who work with them need to be able to communicate their views on why policy changes are needed at national level, as well as being able to communicate their views on the need for changes in policy and practice at the local level.

Differences both within and between areas over time

So far, the focus has been on participants' own evaluations of their experiences of working in partnerships to promote area regeneration. The emphasis has been on the findings which have emerged in common: the recurrent themes and the common agendas. But there were also significant differences of emphasis and perception:

- differences between individuals and groups within the four case study areas;
- differences between the four case study areas;
- differences over time.

Differences between individuals and groups

From the outset, it was recognised that communities are characterised by difference as well as by shared interests. Important differences did indeed emerge, including differences which related to structural inequalities of power – between black and ethnic communities and white communities, between people with middle-class occupations and working-class occupations, between homeowners and tenants, between men and women, between younger people and older people. People's experiences differed significantly and so too did their perspectives, depending on a range of factors.

Differences relating to 'race' and ethnicity

In both the London case studies and in Birmingham, 'race' and ethnicity were key issues. Wherever there were minority communities, there had been problems of exclusion (this theme emerges throughout the previous section). Black and ethnic minority groups voiced a number of serious concerns about the difficulties of engaging in area regeneration partnerships and the lack of effective community work and training support to assist them in doing so more effectively. Although there were major failures in this respect, there were also some examples of positive challenges, such as the effective challenge to exclusive boundaries in Aston/Newtown.

Differences relating to class and tenure

These differences emerged most sharply in the most socially mixed areas – the two London case study areas. The complex structures for community representation, in the Greenwich Waterfront area in particular, contained in-built biases which reproduced inequalities of class and tenure – the voices of working-class tenants were least likely to be heard effectively. In Kings Cross the situation was rather different, because it was complicated by underlying differences of power and perspective between the different partners representing different sectors – private sector property developers with profit-led perspectives on the one hand and local residents' groups and the Kings Cross Railway Lands Group with their alternative vision, on the other.

Other differences

A number of other differences of perspective emerged too, differences which were not being addressed in many cases, because minority voices were not being effectively heard. As one of the professionals in Barnsley commented, "There's a culture of not valuing women and young people". Young people emerged as under-represented in each of the four case study areas (although there were also some examples of successful initiatives to involve young people, such as going out to listen to them rather than assuming that young people are apathetic or even hostile, if they do not attend formal public consultation meetings dominated by official agendas). Young Bangladeshi women in Birmingham gave voice to their experiences of oppression as women, as young people, and as a member of an ethnic minority community (although here too young Bangladeshi women had been challenging their exclusion). Other groups whose voices were not being heard included refugees and asylum seekers, people with disabilities, lesbians and gay men, and homeless people. While there was contention about whether or not homeless people were part of the community, in Kings Cross, also there was evidence of good practice involving homeless people and enabling them to have a voice.

In addition, there were differences relating to people's own experiences and expectations. For example, those who had directly benefited from specific projects and programmes (such as the renovation of their housing, or grants to their local community project) were more likely to be satisfied than those who had not benefited directly. However, people's overall views could not be neatly categorised in this way and those who had started with relatively modest expectations tended to be more satisfied than those with wider aspirations, especially when these wider aspirations raised contentious policy issues and/or development decisions (as in the case of the Kings Cross Railway Lands). Whatever the level of people's aspirations, however, high levels of frustration were expressed, when there was confusion about what was negotiable and what was not.

Differences between the four case study areas

Although there were key similarities and common experiences, there were also important differences between the four case study areas. These included:

- differences in the area's economic infrastructure and the varying issues and underlying interests involved in regeneration;
- differences of political infrastructures and 'cultures';
- differences relating to the previous experiences and present organisational strengths of the voluntary and community sectors;
- differences in the levels of support (including professional and technical advice and support, community work support and training);
- differences between the contributions of particular groups and key individuals.

Differences in the economic infrastructures and varying interests involved

There were considerable differences between the experiences and perspectives of those involved in areas of economic disinvestment and change, such as Barnsley (where professionals and community representatives shared concerns about local economic development) and areas of potential development pressure (such as Kings Cross and Greenwich Waterfront). In the two London case study areas – particularly in Kings Cross – there were significant conflicts of interest around strategic planning issues and major inequalities of power between private property developers and particular local community organisations.

Differences in political 'cultures'

As anticipated, political differences between the

four case study areas were also key and emerged to a significant extent. Some local authorities attracted considerably more criticism than others, being seen as determined to control local partnerships, whatever the rhetoric about the importance of community participation. Participants also identified significant differences within areas and even within the same organisations (community representatives reflected on the variations between particular council departments and even on the variations between teams within the same department, identifying which teams were most responsive to working in partnership with the voluntary and community sectors).

Differences relating to the experiences and organisational strengths of the voluntary and community sectors

There were marked differences here too. The particular experiences of former mining areas, and their histories of organisation and solidarity emerged as significant factors in the more recent strengths of the community sector in Barnsley for example. Similarly in Kings Cross, the previous history of community struggles around strategic planning issues emerged as a significant factor, shaping local awareness of the strategic dimensions (and informing local perceptions of the varying organisations and interests, both positively and negatively).

Differences in the levels of support

Experiences of professional and technical support varied considerably. Negative experiences impacted on the replies in a number of cases. Conversely, where there were positive experiences of relevant support and appropriate training (as in Birmingham and Barnsley) very different responses resulted, both about support and training and about the developing strength of the voluntary and community sectors more generally.

Differences relating to the contributions of particular groups and individuals

The roles of particular groups and individuals emerged as significant in each case study area (whether positively or negatively). Community representatives expressed clear views about who, and which groups or organisations could be relied upon, and conversely professionals expressed similarly clear views about the roles of individuals and particular organisations (again both positively and negatively). In Kings Cross, for example, the appointment of a new chief executive, who was considered to have far more positive views on involving the local community, made a major impact on attitudes towards the partnership, offering new opportunities for reversing some very negative initial experiences.

Differences over time

Communities are also continually changing over time, as are the organisational and wider economic and social policy contexts within which they operate.

Change in individuals and groups

Over time, particular officers and professionals come and go (with positive or negative consequences) and relationships need to be rebuilt. Community activists become more or less involved (so support and training needs to be ongoing if newcomers are to be effectively brought into the process) and organisations become more or less active, with highs and lows of involvement. Similarly the strength and independence of the voluntary and community sector can ebb and flow, processes of change which need to be monitored and evaluated over time. There were also examples of community organisations building up their strength and developing their creativity over time. In South East London, for example, community initiatives had developed, drawing on experiences gained under the City Challenge programme, and the networks which had evolved from these. Communities were researching their own needs and developing bids to run their own programmes.

Political and organisational change

Even within the same political party, the election of a new leadership can have a major impact. In Birmingham, for example, the election of a leader who was known to be strongly committed to decentralisation and community participation was considered to have been a key factor. Here too, such changes can be both positive and negative.

Wider policy changes

Changes in government policies and organisational frameworks have also been key, opening up new opportunities: Chapter 1 summarised some of the most significant of these opportunities. Conversely, constant change can have destabilising effects (for example, replacing one set of structures to fit the requirements of the latest statutory framework, just as these become established, and refocusing community priorities to fit the latest funding criteria). One Barnsley community development worker commented that this felt like, "government by initiatives". If the lessons of community participation in area regeneration programmes are not built into these wider policy changes, the prospects for future partnerships may be significantly undermined.

Conclusions and recommendations

Participatory monitoring and evaluation: community research and development

This research started by asking questions about how participants evaluated the lessons of their experiences of participation in area regeneration programmes, how they evaluated the support that had been available to them and how they evaluated their own impact. The researchers were actually struck by how few opportunities participants had been offered to do precisely this – how few opportunities there were for critical reflection. It was widely recognised by participants that the pace of initiatives, the demands on people's time and the conflicting pressures representatives were placed under, combined to create a situation where there very few *safe spaces* in which participatory monitoring and evaluation could take place. When participants were offered such opportunities through the research, the response was overwhelmingly positive. Even very busy community representatives and activists, made time to participate in the research; and many commented on the value of taking part in these processes, both individually and collectively. Opportunities for sharing experiences and reflections were especially valued – particularly when community representatives and activists came together with professionals from the four case study areas. The researchers would like to reiterate their appreciation of the time which so many busy people gave, and the support which they provided, both to the research team and to other participants.

This finding is significant in itself: participants have vital contributions to make – both about processes and outcomes in area regeneration

programmes and about the policy and resource allocation implications at local, regional and national levels. This is more important than ever in the current policy context. As Chapter 1 argued, the involvement of communities is high on the policy agenda, both in relation to the developing National Strategy for Neighbourhood Renewal (SEU, 1999a) and in relation to tackling social exclusion within mainstream programmes more generally. There are also key implications for local governance, including the development of Community Plans and for regional agendas and the regional development agencies.

From the outset, the research questioned how far participants' experiences and views might vary, depending on their own values and perspectives and on factors such as their gender, age, ethnicity, occupation or lack of paid work, and their previous organisational experiences. This research reinforced the importance of the aspects of diversity and difference – communities are not homogenous. The ways in which different voices were expressed – and heard or not heard – raised central issues about representation and accountability. It is more important than ever to address these issues in the context of new agendas for local and regional governance.

Participatory monitoring and evaluation needs to start from this recognition of the importance of representing diversity and difference. Participatory monitoring and evaluation needs to be built into area regeneration programmes and appropriately resourced before bids are even agreed, and similar processes need to be developed in comparable programmes, both small area programmes and mainstream community planning programmes. The audit tools provide one key mechanism – a set of tools to facilitate participatory monitoring and evaluation of processes as well as outputs and outcomes. The report also identified other tools, including those which have been created through participatory approaches in developing nations.

While emphasising the potential value of such tools, it is also important to emphasise that there are no simple solutions and no pat answers to the dilemmas inherent in community participation in regeneration and development. These tools are just that: tools to produce greater transparency, to enable participants to gain clearer knowledge and critical understanding about who is gaining what, about who is failing to gain, who is losing out, and about how processes and outcomes can be challenged.

From the research in the four case study areas, we found impressive evidence of the range of participants' knowledge, skills and critical understanding. People reflected on their learning both as individuals and in groups. This knowledge was applied in practice and there were powerful examples to illustrate people's energy, determination and sheer creativity in practice. There were also examples of how people had mounted effective challenges to official agendas, policies and practices. These examples included challenges to communities' initial experiences of exclusion; for example, the Bangladeshi Youth Forum's successful challenge has already illustrated this in the context of the boundary issues in Aston/Newtown in Birmingham.

There were also examples where communities were becoming their own researchers, analysing their own needs and developing their own strategies to meet these needs. Despite the inherent difficulties in working within area regeneration programmes, communities were taking the initiative to develop their own agendas.

There were also examples of communities developing strategies for sustainable development, taking into account the diversity of needs, interests and perspectives. We have already looked at examples of development trusts in Barnsley with sustainable assets emerging from community forums: Acorn, Grimethorpe, has been quoted as an example of a sustainable asset which was created out of previous regeneration programmes. People in this area valued the continuing support provided to community activity and commented on the centre's atmosphere which was warm and welcoming to local people.

Combating exclusion: Somerstown, Kings Cross

When the original boundary was drawn for the Kings Cross Partnership (KCP) area it cut through the Somerstown area so that one half benefited from SRB designation and the other half did not. Partly in response, local residents and groups organised through a new structure, the Somerstown and St Pancras Steering Group to ensure that the KCP boundary was extended and to secure more SRB funds through a community-led bid supported by the local council and KCP.

Communities as researchers: New Cross Community Research Project, South East London

The New Cross Community Research Project was developed by a partnership of local organisations who succeeded in gaining Adult and Community Learning Fund resources in 1998 to support local people develop their own community-based regeneration bid for the area. Local people have been supported and provided with appropriate training to enable them to research the range of local needs and priorities. This community-based research has been linked with extensive consultation, using a variety of different approaches to ensure that there is a strong sense of community ownership among the diverse sections of the local community. This applies both to the research and to the resulting SRB bid.

Community-based agendas for sustainability: Pepys Community Forum, South East London

In 1997, agencies and residents in Pepys, South East London, began meeting to look at ways of improving the quality of life and services for people living in the area. The Pepys Community Forum developed out of these initiatives and put its own community regeneration bid together, via Lewisham Council. The bid was successful, wining SRB5 funding to deliver community-based services and, over the coming six years, to develop a Community Development Trust. Through this trust, Pepys Community Forum will be able to continue delivering community-based services to meet local needs into the future. Working parties are currently identifying priority needs around children and young people, childcare, healthy living, local economic development and community arts.

Policy debates

Chapter 1 identified three areas of contemporary policy debates as having particular relevance to this report. The findings speak directly to each of these debates.

Social capital

'Social capital' can be used as a term which focuses on the 'local cultures' of particular communities in negative ways, measuring the degrees to which people lack this commodity. Such a stance can promote policy initiatives around capacity building that are premised on a cultural deficit model, assuming that particular communities are deficient and hence in need of being supplied with social capital. As such, the cultural deficit approach begins to echo some of the assumptions which were expressed in debates about *cultures of poverty* in the 1960s and 1970s. In contrast, our findings reinforce the importance of focusing and building on the strengths of particular communities. Contemporary debates on social capital need to be set in the context of specific historical and geographical understandings of the development of community and third sector *networks* in particular areas, positively as well as negatively. In all four case study areas the strengths and weaknesses of such networks were strongly related to the strengths and the weaknesses of community participation. In each of the case studies social capital could be understood in terms of group and individual relationships to such network structures as these developed over time.

This finding in turn relates to agendas for Lifelong Learning and Learning for Active Citizenship (as set out in DfEE, 1998). Both individuals and groups had clearly been learning through their experiences of community participation. Individuals had been acquiring knowledge and skills and gaining confidence; some were going on to further study leading to professional and other vocational qualifications. Groups and organisations had also been learning through their experiences of participation in active citizenship. Through the development of participatory monitoring and evaluation systems, with safe spaces for reflection and critical analysis, these opportunities for learning and for the associated development of social capital could be significantly enhanced.

The 'local' in small area programmes

There can be no simple 'territorial' definitions underpinning small area programmes – there will inevitably be some occasions on which the proliferation of different zones, areas and borders will create overlapping governance structures. Boundaries invariably create issues around who is excluded and who included in particular funding regimes. It is not plausible to imagine a situation where the boundaries of health provisions, criminal justice regimes, local authority areas, labour markets, economic sub-regions and travel-to-work areas could ever be coterminous. Consequently it is important to develop an understanding of the processes by which different local area regeneration initiatives *define* communities in terms of particular places and develop representative structures that are flexible to the multiple 'territories' of governance that emerge as a result.

Democracy, the democratic deficit and the reform of governance at local and regional levels

The current policy agenda recognises that a plurality of interests needs to be represented in structures of local governance. The democratic franchise is only one form of such representation and, by itself, is not always best suited to producing an effective community voice in small area initiatives. Logically, new democratic structures need to develop additional forms of representation that acknowledge the status of different interest groups; the network, the particular individual, the specific interest, the major and minor stakeholders all define 'communities' distinctively and each may have a legitimate and important contribution to a small area regeneration programme. However, the processes by which communities are represented are problematic – as experiences in the four case study areas demonstrate. Thus it is vitally important to pay greater attention to the processes by which the representation of communities is defined in small area regeneration programmes and to develop flexible methods of representing the complexity of community structures in ways which are effectively accountable.

While these findings are particularly relevant to democratic representation within small area regeneration programmes, they have relevance within the wider policy context at regional and national levels. The recognition of the neighbourhood as a central dynamic within society is clearly at the heart of the work of the SEU and its stress on the importance of a National Strategy for Neighbourhood Renewal (SEU, 1999a). However, the value of this emphasis on the neighbourhood should not undermine the importance of the other geographical scales. The clear differences between the problems of area regeneration highlighted in this report – inside and outside London – point to the continued significance of the regional agenda within the UK (and in relation to European agendas). This reinforces the importance of developing effective and democratically accountable forms of representation both at the community level and beyond, within cities and regions. Debates on regional devolution need to emphasise the importance of developing and sustaining appropriate vehicles of community representation within the new structures of regional governance.

Significant connections between the research findings and key findings emerging from the SEU Policy Action Teams' reports

The delivery of a National Strategy for Neighbourhood Renewal by the SEU (1999a) is clearly of major significance for this research. This section highlights the relationships between these research findings and some of the key findings of both the Policy Action Teams (PATs) and the outline national strategy.

Policy Action Team 9 (Community Self-help)

PAT 9's findings are particularly relevant to the findings of this report. This is especially evident in the following recommendations. PAT 9:

- emphasise that community self-help is a complement to, not a substitute for, effective public services; and it must be activity done by local communities, not for or to them;
- acknowledge that every community is different and consequently emphasise that it is essential to 'work with the grain' of local specificity and 'build on what is there';
- stress the significance of developing local action plans for community self-help; we would also suggest that these be built into the process of community planning (examined below);
- acknowledge that people learn most effectively from their peers – as our findings on training in area regeneration indicate; we

would further suggest that customised training models for capacity building are far more likely to succeed in enhancing voluntary sector activity unlike some output-focused, standard models of training;
- encourage funders to provide dedicated funding to support the infrastructure of the black and minority ethnic voluntary sector and be prepared to fund them to become local service providers.

Policy Action Team 5 (Housing Management) and Policy Action Team 7 (Unpopular Housing)

PATs 5 and 7 recognise the complexity of local communities through their emphasis of the importance of tenant involvement in the management of social housing. They recognise that it is important that such participation complements rather than generates conflict with other 'community stakeholders' in models of community participation in area regeneration.

In addition, PAT 7 recommends that the local authority role in addressing issues of unpopular housing should be strengthened. This recommendation raises policy issues which have already emerged from this research, with wider implications for addressing the causes of the residualisation of social housing. This, in turn, raises questions about the need for structures and processes for scaling up and mainstreaming, drawing on the lessons of community participation in small area regeneration programmes, feeding policy changes from the bottom up, to regional and national levels, as well as from the top downwards.

Policy implementation

The research points to some key policy implementation issues that need to be addressed to strengthen the inclusion of community perspectives into area regeneration programmes. While these recommendations are specifically geared towards area regeneration programmes, many have broader relevance for community participation in a range of related policy areas, at local, regional and national levels.

In drawing out these policy implementation issues, this report reinforces the importance of guidance for SRB bids, as set out in the Joseph

Rowntree Foundation paper 'Developing effective community involvement strategies'. These guidelines set the framework, starting from the importance of:

- 'getting started' (building on local community knowledge, skills and priorities);
- 'involving communities in partnerships' (with appropriate resourcing and training);
- 'creating strong local organisations with their own assets' (such as development trusts);
- 'developing an infrastructure to build and sustain community organisations';
- monitoring progress (including both outputs and processes).

The audit tools have key relevance here as they provide a mechanism by which government, at national and regional levels, can assess and evaluate the extent to which bids are incorporating effective processes of community participation. The audit tools also provide a mechanism by which the different stakeholders can proceed to monitor and evaluate participation processes over time. From the outset, community representatives and activists, professionals and decision makers in the relevant structures need to develop agreements which can form the basis for participatory monitoring and evaluation, using the audit tools to measure processes as well as outputs and outcomes at regular intervals throughout the life of each area regeneration programme.

There needs to be sufficient time to develop dialogues with communities

The annual rounds for area regeneration programme bidding mean that time represents an overarching barrier which inhibits stakeholders from developing dialogues on the design, implementation, monitoring and evaluation of programmes. Lack of time is a particular barrier to:

- developing and agreeing basic programme objectives and appropriate outcome and monitoring criteria;
- implementing strategies for engagement with a wide range of community perspectives throughout the life of the spending programme;
- reaching out, inclusively, to all sections of the community – including those groups and individuals not previously engaged with formal

community;
- developing and agreeing plans for appropriate support and training for all those involved;
- providing opportunities for reflection on the lessons learned, within and between programmes, including reflecting on processes as well as overall outcomes.

Recent changes to SRB and New Deal for Communities bidding guidance have addressed the issue of time, but this needs to be taken further. The proposal for the 'Year Zero' – a year for joint preparation and planning to identify, needs and strategic priorities – needs to be implemented effectively.

The case studies – in common with other studies – have also suggested that there has been insufficient flexibility in SRB programming, limiting the scope to respond to community needs as these develop over time. Contingency provision must be made in area-based programme spending to allow for this.

The key importance of resources, including resources for independent technical and professional advice

Practice on the ground suggests that the structures and support mechanisms which are available at local level are not generally sufficient to facilitate the development of community-led agendas and projects. The provision of effective infrastructures of independent support and technical aid at regional and local levels is particularly uneven; this has not been 'required' provision and has therefore remained an optional extra. There need to be agreed standards for good practice, and these need to be set out in written codes of good practice for local authorities, regeneration agencies and regional governance structures.

Impact on the community sector more generally: strengthening social capital or reinforcing the effective exclusion of the least resourced community groups?

Evidence from the case studies suggests that community participation in area-based programmes can have negative as well as positive impacts on the community sector. A 'social Darwinism' effect on the community and voluntary sector can be observed – a form of the 'survival of the fittest' – as those who are able develop the knowledge and skills to negotiate the guidelines and procedures of regeneration funding 'win out' over smaller or less experienced groups (particularly unfunded groups with no paid staff or professional support workers). The impact of area regeneration programmes on the overall strength and independence of the community sector did not form part of the formal evaluation of programmes in any of the four case study areas. This was an important omission, which needs to be addressed in future monitoring and evaluation strategies.

Integration with mainstream programmes

This research has demonstrated that participants perceive their lack of involvement in policy and resource allocation decisions of mainstream service providers (such as local authorities, health authorities and education and training providers) as a significant issue. This emerged as a negative feature in their evaluation of area regeneration programmes. Similar criticisms apply to the lack of interface with policies and resource allocation decisions at both regional and national levels. Participants also raised the issue of substitution (of mainstream spending with area-based programmes). In addition, they questioned the value of setting up projects that turned out to unsustainable, because there were inadequate mechanisms for integrating these into mainstream programmes.

The changing agenda for local governance could provide opportunities to address these issues through the development of community plans. These could provide the focus for negotiating about strategic regeneration objectives, and about the relations between strategic objectives and local area-based initiatives. The development of regional strategies (linked to the new regional structures and regional development agencies) makes the relationships between these different levels all the more significant. Many participants expressed scepticism about agendas for community planning, precisely because of their negative experience of participation in regeneration structures in the past. Local community planning structures need to learn these lessons and regional structures need to be developed in ways that take them into account.

Implications for changes in local governance and the development of community plans

Current government thinking, as expressed in the White Paper, *Modernising local government: In touch with the people* (DETR, 1998) suggests a new role for local authorities based on the notion that:

> community leadership is at the heart of the role of modern local government. Councils are the organizations best placed to take a comprehensive overview of the needs and priorities of their local areas and communities and lead the work to meet those needs and practices in the round. (DETR, 1998, p 79)

The proposed general power for local authorities to assume a "responsibility for the well-being and sustainable development of its area" (DETR, 1998, p 80) represents a potentially significant change in the relationship between local authorities and local communities. These changes relate to the perceived need for local authorities to achieve renewed legitimacy. Research for this report highlighted both the potential for this to occur and the degrees of cynicism and disillusionment with which democratically-elected local councils are viewed in some places. Renewed legitimacy for local councils will be significantly related to the effectiveness with which these new powers are exercised – particularly in relation to community planning. Lessons can be learnt from participants' experiences of participation in area regeneration. Participation in community planning needs to start from the same principles as community participation in area regeneration programmes, as set out in this report and the accompanying recommendations (Burns and Taylor, 2000). Participation in community planning needs to be monitored and evaluated in comparable ways, drawing from the audit tools.

- Community planning must begin from a critical examination of the processes of consultation and participation currently adopted by the local authority (in different areas of council service delivery and in sub-authority or 'neighbourhood' forums or arenas).
- The different *representative interests* in the locality need to be distinguished and appropriate measures taken, to facilitate contributions from these different interests. Community planning must involve *coordination* between major public sector

players in an area (such as the police, higher education and health services). It must also involve developing the *aspirations* of local neighbourhood interests and clarifying the *strategic interests* of the authority itself, as well as those of private sector stakeholders whose concerns may involve very different sets of power relations.

- The creation of appropriate processes for participation for these different 'community stakeholders' needs to be prioritised. The best means for inter-agency working between major public sector players is not the same as the appropriate means to engage the private sector in discussion. In turn, these will be different from engaging in dialogue with networks of individual concerns at neighbourhood level. Community planning must consequently match *participatory functions* with appropriate *participatory forms* which acknowledge these differences.

- There needs to be adequate acknowledgement of the fact that community planning takes place in the context of other medium- and long-term planning processes for key service areas of the local authority (such as the Education Development Plan) and for the plans of other private and public sector players in the locality.

- There needs to be clarity about *what is at stake*. At the outset, it is essential to determine those issues where local communities are to be *consulted on specific proposals* being made by local authorities and those issues where communities are being invited to *participate in defining the proposals* in the first place or to *make decisions* on alternative options. For example, there is no point in local authorities working in a community safety partnership with other community safety interests if the budgetary commitments are not made explicit by all parties concerned. Equally, there is no point in consulting with local communities when decisions have already been made or on matters where the aspirations of neighbourhood groups are – for whatever reasons – impossible to realise.

- There needs to be acknowledgement that the rules of representative democracy are those which structure local authority activity, but they are not necessarily those that facilitate the most effective community contributions. This needs to be acknowledged by other stakeholders too, whether private sector interests or voluntary sector organisations.

Towards good practice

Examples of good practice in community participation could be identified in all four case study areas, but what was notable was the extreme 'patchiness' of these examples of good practice. Too often, these were dependent on specific individuals or particular projects with access to key resources such as independent technical advice, relevant training and community development support. The level of support from particular local authorities was also variable. Some very basic barriers to participation still exist – lack of accessible information, inappropriate times of meetings, lack of childcare provision, lack of transparency in decision making, and lack of tangible results from the process.

The case studies suggest that the diversity of community interests is insufficiently recognised, and resources are not systematically allocated to address this diversity. This typically remains an unallocated responsibility. Addressing issues of diversity was all too often seen as 'difficult', and there were generally inadequate resources for the intensive outreach work which is often necessary to reach the most under-represented groups. In three of the four case study areas, where there were black and ethnic minority communities, there were major issues to be addressed. As Chapter 3 has already demonstrated, there were also issues around the under-representation of a range of other groups and interests within communities, despite some examples of good practice.

The audit tools, which have been developed as part of this study, provide a mechanism for addressing these issues, providing a framework for stakeholders to monitor and evaluate these aspects of community participation. This will assist in the task of levelling the differences in the quality of community participation in area-based programmes and developing the necessary systems and processes to ensure that community participation becomes more genuinely inclusive as well as becoming more democratically accountable, more effective and more influential.

Recommendations

Government regeneration programmes

A comprehensive community involvement strategy should be developed in area regeneration programmes and funding decisions should, in part, depend on assessments of the quality of these strategies. Area regeneration partnerships should develop 'charters' of community involvement that draw on good practice advice, including the 'Guidance for Single Regeneration Budget bids: developing effective community involvement strategies', and these 'charters' should be subjected to independent evaluation. The audit tools provide a mechanism for assessing bids, and then facilitating participatory processes of monitoring and evaluation. Capacity building should be a key goal of area regeneration programmes and this priority should be reflected in resource allocation decisions.

More specifically government programmes should:

- **Provide sufficient time and resources**, including independent technical aid, to enable communities to develop their own agendas (including increased time and resources for communities to do this during Year Zero development periods, with contingency fund programmes, for use during the period of the programme, to respond to changing circumstances).
- **Incorporate increased resources for participation and capacity building** as part of the requirements for bidding (and require that proposals for participation and capacity building are adequate before bids can be agreed). (This might normally be expected to represent a minimum of 10% of the overall budget for any particular programme.)
- **Develop a national framework for supporting learnning**, technical aid and training, opening pathways for progression both for communities and for the relevant professionals; require appropriate targets to be set, and resources ring-fenced to meet these targets, before bids can be agreed.
- **Require that bids include comprehensive training and learning strategies**, starting from participants' own analyses of their learning needs on a continuing basis. These strategies to include both formal learning and courses and informal learning (including mentoring schemes and exchange visits between communities developing comparable programmes and projects) targeted to meet the needs of individuals and groups. Learning strategies should also include opportunities for bringing community representatives and professionals together for joint training. These strategies should include opportunities for accreditation and progression, both for individuals and for groups and organisations.
- **Require that appropriate and effective participatory monitoring and evaluation systems be developed** (including the use of audit tools to measure processes as well as outputs) before bids can be agreed.
- **Sponsor the development of models of participatory monitoring and evaluation** including monitoring and evaluation of the changing impact of area regeneration programmes, of the strength and independence of the community sector and the impact on the development of social capital more generally.
- **Provide resources to enable community representatives to network** regionally and nationally to share experiences and findings **and to make recommendations to government** at both regional and national levels (including recommendations about the implications for national and regional policies and resource allocation decisions).
- **Develop structures at both regional and national levels to enable such findings and recommendations to be received and taken into consideration.**

Government Offices, Regional Development Agencies and partnerships

Regional structures of governance may not have been designed to 'represent' the complexities of local communities per se. However, by demanding better practice from local authorities in area regeneration programmes and other small area initiatives they can and should be instrumental in enhancing the representativeness and legitimacy of local democracy. In addition, regional structures need to develop their own mechanisms for promoting community participation at regional level, and for building in mechanisms for scaling up and mainstreaming; drawing on the lessons of community participation at local level.

A minimum figure of 5% of funding should be reserved for the independent evaluation of community participation in area regeneration programmes, with reporting structures that guarantee that the findings of these evaluations are made available to all stakeholders in the regeneration process.

More specifically Government Offices and Regional Development Agencies and partnerships should:

- **Adopt the use of the audit tools as part of a consistent approach to evaluating community participation** in area regeneration programmes, including processes as well as outcomes and outputs.
- **Develop regional strategies for the provision of technical advice, independent consultancy and training** with regional resources – and regional databases – to facilitate access to effective technical expertise and advice, consultancy, training and learning opportunities. These should include opportunities for joint training between community representatives, professionals and decision makers, and there should be opportunities for accreditation and progression.
- **Ensure that sources of technical advice, independent consultancy, community support and learning support are readily available** (for example via regional consortia) with accessible opportunities for individuals and groups to develop their knowledge and skills, including skills as community researchers (and consultants in their own right) and to gain accreditation for these.

Local authorities and local regeneration agencies

Participants in the case study areas generally saw local authorities as key stakeholders with the power to make or break community participation in regeneration partnerships. Alongside local regeneration agencies, local authority officers and members have vital roles to play.

More specifically local authorities and local regeneration agencies should:

- **Ensure that all bids include appropriate provision for community participation** including independent advice and support and training, and for participatory monitoring and evaluation (including through use of the audit tools).

- **Ensure that practical support is available** (including the costs of childcare and transport) to enable people to participate, valuing people's time and paying for this where appropriate.
- **Disseminate examples of good practice**, supporting initiatives to enable communities to develop their own projects and their own community-based partnership bids.
- **Take shared responsibility to ensure that the range of community views are being heard** and to ensure that structures for community participation are both representative and democratically accountable.
- **Require that the impact of area regeneration on the community sector is effectively monitored** and that appropriate action is taken, where necessary, to strengthen the community sector and safeguard its independent voice.
- **Provide support for the community sector to facilitate participatory monitoring** and evaluation and to facilitate networking at local and regional levels, to share experience and findings.
- **Develop strategies to ensure that the changing role of local councillors takes account of the requirements of the community sector.**

Community sector organisations

Community organisations and networks within area regeneration programmes should establish clear goals and action plans for their involvement and these goals should be built into the 'charters' recommended. Just as government funding of regeneration programmes should be dependent on effective local plans for community involvement, community sector and voluntary sector agencies should similarly promote transparency through the independent evaluation of initiatives carried out by third sector organisations. The funding of networks of community and voluntary sector activity should, in addition, be used to facilitate the contributions of third sector organisations to processes of community planning, as developed by local authorities more generally.

More specifically community organisations and groups should:

- **Share responsibility for ensuring that community participation structures are**

genuinely inclusive, representative and democratically accountable, taking account of minority as well as majority interests.

- **Participate in identifying their own support and learning needs** on a continuing basis.
- **Participate in the planning and delivery of learning programmes** (including participating in joint sessions with professionals).
- **Participate in providing support within their own organisations and communities** (for example, briefing/debriefing others in the community, including new members of community organisations and partnership boards).
- **Participate in the provision of mentoring** for new members/board members.
- **Participate in networking and community exchanges.**
- **Share experiences and learning** within their own organisations and with organisations and groups with common interests in their area and beyond.
- **Share responsibility for participatory monitoring and evaluation**, taking account of the wider impact on the community sector (realistically taking account of constraints of time and other resources).
- **Strengthen networks** between community sector organisations locally and regionally, sharing experiences and buildings alliances around shared interests and concerns.

References

Barnes, C. and Mercer, G. (eds) (1997) *Doing disability research*, Leeds: The Disability Press.

Burns, D. and Taylor, M. (2000) *Auditing community participation: An assessment handbook*, Bristol/York: The Policy Press/JRF.

Clapham, D. (1996) 'Residents' attitudes and perceptions: position paper', York: JRF.

Cloke, C. and Davies, M. (eds) (1995) *Participation and empowerment in child protection*, London: Pitman.

DETR (Department of the Environment, Transport and the Regions) (1998) *Modern local government: In touch with the people*, London: The Stationery Office.

DfEE (Department for Education and Employment) (1998) *The Learning Age: A renaissance for a new Britain*, Green Paper, London: The Stationery Office.

Estrella, M and Gaventa, J. (1998) *Who counts reality? Participatory, monitoring and evaluation: A literature review*, Brighton: Institute of Development Studies.

Fitzpatrick, S., Hastings, A. and Kintrea, K. (1998) *Including young people in urban regeneration: A lot to learn?*, Bristol: The Policy Press.

Gilchrist, A. and Taylor, M. (1997) 'Community networking: developing strength through diversity', in P. Hoggett (ed) *Contested communities: Experiences, struggles, policies*, Bristol: The Policy Press, pp 165-79.

Guijt, I. and Shah, M. (eds) (1998) *The myth of community: Gender issues in participatory development*, London: Intermediate Technology.

Hasting, A., McArthur, A.A. and McGregor, A. (1996) *Less than equal? Community organisations and estate regeneration partnerships*, Bristol/York: The Policy Press/JRF.

Hastings, A. and McArthur, A.A. (1995) 'A comparative assessment of government approaches to partnership with the local community', in R. Hambleton and H. Thomas (eds) *Urban policy evaluation*, London: Paul Chapman, pp 175-93.

Henderson, P. and Mayo, M. (1998) *Training and education in urban regeneration: A framework for participants*, Bristol/York: The Policy Press/ JRF.

Holland, J. et al (eds) *Whose voice?*, London: Intermediate Technology.

Joseph Rowntree Foundation (1999) 'Guidance for Single Regeneration Budget bids: developing effective community involvement strategies', York: JRF.

Lindow, V. and Morris, J. (1995) *Service user involvement: Synthesis of findings and experiences in the field of community care*, York: JRF.

Schofield, G. and Thoburn, J. (1996) *Child protection: The voice of the child*, London: Institute of Public Policy Research.

SEU* (Social Exclusion Unit) (1999a) *Bringing Britain together: A national strategy for neighbourhood renewal*, London: Cabinet Office.

SEU* (1999b) *Enterprise and social exclusion*, Policy Action Team 3 Report, London: Cabinet Office.

SEU* (1999c) *Housing management*, Report by Policy Action Team 5 published for consultation by the DETR, London: Cabinet Office.

SEU* (1999d) *Unpopular housing*, Report by Policy Action Team 7 published for consultation by the DETR, London: Cabinet Office.

SEU* (1999e) *Community self-help*, Report by Policy Action Team 9 published for consultation by the Home Office, London: Cabinet Office

Taylor, M. (1995) *Unleashing the potential*, York: JRF.

Wilson, G. (ed) (1995) *Community care: Asking the users*, London: Chapman and Hall.

Note: * For all SEU reports and relevant hyperlinks see http://www.cabinet-office.uk/seu/index.htm

Appendix: Auditing community participation

This Appendix is an extract from *Auditing community participation*, by the Audit Tools team (Burns and Taylor, 2000).

Why audit community participation?

Partnership is a central theme of government policy today. There is also an increasing commitment to community participation and community-led partnerships. But partnership and community involvement are not new; and despite successive regeneration initiatives, all the evidence suggests that, in the past, there has been a considerable gap between rhetoric and reality. Even now communities and their representatives often feel marginalised – on the edges of power. There have been a number of reasons for this, but briefly, the evidence suggests that:

- the 'rules of the game' are set from above;
- the cultures and structures of public sector partners are not compatible with effective community involvement;
- communities themselves do not have the organisational capacity and resources for effective involvement.

Some of the lessons from the past are being learnt through the New Deal for Communities and the more recent rounds of the Single Regeneration Budget. They are also enshrined in the proposed National Strategy for Neighbourhood Renewal, where neighbourhood residents are seen as crucial.

> The involvement and leadership of local people is vital to turning round deprived neighbourhoods and helping them to thrive. (SEU, 2000, para 4.10./2)

However, there is still a lot of variation in the practice of partnerships around the country and across the different departments of public authorities. What can be done to ensure that public bodies and others involved in partnerships give more priority to community involvement? How can we be sure that the rhetoric of partnership with communities is translated into effective practice?

One thing that public bodies and partnerships do take seriously is the need to account for public money through financial audit. Over the years the need to account for public money has influenced the ways that public bodies are structured and the systems and procedures that they set up. It has also influenced the way that partnerships are designed and run. If a similarly rigorous account had to be given of the measures taken to encourage community involvement, would this ensure that public authorities and partnerships were structured in ways that facilitated genuine participation and took community issues and views on board?

Why should communities participate?

One of the reasons communities are marginalised is because partners are not convinced of the value of participation. It is worth, therefore, rehearsing the arguments for community participation.

Why is community participation essential?

- Community definitions of need, problems and solutions are different from those put forward by service planners and providers.

- Community knowledge is an important resource, and widens the pool of experience and expertise that regeneration and renewal strategies can draw on.

- Community participation gives local residents the opportunity to develop skills and networks that they need to address social exclusion.

- Active participation of local residents is essential to improved democratic and service accountability.

- Central government requires community participation in regeneration and neighbourhood renewal strategies.

Is audit relevant to community participation?

At first glance, the idea of applying audit mechanisms to community participation may seem fraught with difficulties.

First, public bodies and partnerships already have to deal with ever-growing demands for regulation, recording and monitoring. Is further regulation and audit the way to encourage more effective practice in community participation? Or does it simply add to a system of carrots and sticks that inhibit effective action and take time away from the front line? It is clear from research that bureaucracy acts as a barrier to participation. Would a community participation audit stifle the very processes it is meant to encourage?

Second, the culture of audit appears to run counter to many of the principles that underpin community participation. Audit is based on rules and measures. It is task oriented and specific, often based on quantitative measures imposed from the outside. Community participation, on the other hand, needs to be based on trust. It is about processes and learning – building quality in rather than testing it out. Neighbourhood renewal and regeneration are complex processes – there are no simple solutions. Effective partnerships with communities, some argue, need to be flexible and to have the room to evolve rather than being based on the tried and the tested. (For a discussion of the evolutionary nature of partnerships, see Pratt et al, 1999.)

Audit	Community participation
Rules	Trust
Risk averse	Flexible
Quantitative	Qualitative
Task driven	Value driven
External control	Autonomy

However, Ed Mayo of the New Economics Foundation (NEF/Volprof, 1996) suggests that audit has the following strengths. It is:

- comprehensive;
- regular;
- comparative;
- externally validated;
- transparent.

These strengths have been recognised in the growing movement over recent years to introduce social audits into public and private organisations. Social audit is used to check how far organisations are achieving objectives other than the financial bottom line, such as equal opportunities and environmental sustainability.

In adapting traditional audit mechanisms to new objectives, social audits have developed other characteristics. Social audit aims to:

- draw on many perspectives, not just one;
- reflect local circumstances – for example, political context, organisational capacity;
- encourage enquiry and learning;
- be peer driven rather than top-down;
- be qualitative rather than just quantitative.

Approached in this way, audit can be used positively to **facilitate** learning and dialogue, rather than as a stick to beat those who have not yet learnt how to perform effectively or jump through the right hoops. It can be done in partnership rather than imposed from the top-down.

However, developing this approach to auditing community participation does throw up a number of challenges.

First, ways of auditing would need to be found to reflect the **diversity** within communities, the time it takes to involve these diverse communities and the dynamics of involvement. There are likely to be waves or **cycles of involvement**, according to the stage of partnership and the significance of the issues it is addressing. Second, ways of auditing would also need to reflect the different starting points and pressures on different partners. In particular, they would need to take account of the **complexity** of accountability within partnerships – the fact that different partners are accountable to different bodies and constituencies for different things. Third, they would need to understand and find ways of expressing the 'intangibles' of community involvement and to find **simple measures for complex processes** – measures that would be meaningful to all the partners without reducing participation to a lowest common denominator.

It is important that a participation audit should not be another set of measures imposed on communities and their partners from above. Simplistic indicators set from outside the local situation encourage people to find ways of avoiding them. If community participation is to be audited, the tools that are used need to be something that all partners in participating communities can use and that can be jointly owned.

Developing an audit tool

A study funded by the Joseph Rowntree Foundation and carried out by researchers at Goldsmiths' College, University of London, has been evaluating community involvement in previous regeneration schemes – particularly City Challenge and Single Regeneration Budget Partnerships. Although there was variation between the case study partnerships that were studied, the research found that residents still felt

that the power in partnerships lay elsewhere and that they were on the margins of partnership.

As part of this study, researchers from the Universities of Brighton and Bristol explored the possibility of developing a tool for auditing community involvement. They began by carrying out three group discussions with residents and community representatives currently involved in the partnerships being studied by the Goldsmiths' team. The purpose of these discussions was to find out what community participants in partnerships thought were important indicators of community participation. The researchers then drew on these discussions and on previous research to design an initial set of audit tools. They then ran two further groups – one with community representatives, one with local authority officers – to find out how useful they thought the tools might be. The attached set of 'audit tools' is the product of that process. While designed for regeneration partnerships, the tools could be used for other initiatives that require public bodies to engage with communities.

Designing audit

The design of the audit tools needed to address four key questions:

- What to measure?
- How to measure it?
- What the measures offer to those engaged in partnerships?
- Who should do the measuring?

Building on the earlier discussion, we were looking for something that would ask simple but meaningful questions, that would be easy to use, that would be useful and relevant to all the stakeholders and that would have credibility.

What to measure

The audit tools are grouped under five headings. The initial section is designed to establish the context within which participation is being introduced.

The next three sections ask what needs to be in place for community participation to be effective. These questions are based on the three problem areas that we identified at the beginning of this introduction, and aim to establish whether

1 Mapping the history and pattern of participation

	Key question	Indicator
A	What is the range and level of local community activity?	Partners have a clear picture of the range and levels of community participation which already exist.
B	What communities are there within the localities covered by the partnership?	Partners have a clear picture of the different communities that may wish to participate.
C	What local barriers are there to participation?	Partners are aware of the barriers to participation and have considered how they might be addressed.

2 The quality of participation strategies adopted by partners and partnerships

	Key question	Indicator
1a	Who or what has determined the rules of the partnership?	Local communities are involved as equal partners in setting the rules and agendas for the partnership.
1b	What is the balance of power within the partnership?	Communities have as much power and influence as other key stakeholders.
2a	Where in the process are communities involved?	Communities are involved in all aspects of the partnership process.
2b	How much influence/control do communities have?	Communities are given the opportunity to have effective influence and control.
3a	What investment is made in developing and sustaining community participation?	Partnerships invest significant time, money and resources in developing participation.
3b	How strong is the leadership within partnerships and partner organisations?	There is long-term, committed and skilled leadership for participation within the partnership and partner organisations.
4	Does the community participation strategy allow for a variety of 'ways in'?	(a) A variety of different approaches to participation are being tried. (b) Attention is paid to strengthening all forms of community participation.

3 The capacity within partner organisations to support community participation

5	Can decisions be taken at neighbourhood level?	Decisions can be taken at a level that local communities can influence.
6	Do decision-making structures allow for local diversity?	Neighbourhoods/localities can be different from one another.
7	Are services 'joined up'?	Partner organisations can deliver integrated solutions to problems.
8	Are service structures compatible with community participation?	Service structures, boundaries and timetables are compatible with neighbourhood and community structures, boundaries and timetables

4 The capacity within communities to participate effectively

9 How accessible are local meetings?	Local community groups are accessible to potential members.
10 Are community groups able to run in an effective and inclusive way?	Local groups work in an effective, open and inclusive way.
11 How do groups ensure that their representatives are accountable?	Representatives are accountable and have the power to make decisions.

5 Impact assessments

12 How effective is participatory decision making?	(a) Issues of importance to the community get onto agendas. (b) Decisions made by the community are implemented.
13 What are the outcomes of participation?	Outcomes result from participation that would not have happened if participation had not occured.
14 Who benefits from participation?	(a) Opportunities are provided for all sections of the community to participate. (b) Participation benefits all sections of the community.

adequate systems and processes are in place to ensure that the participation can be achieved. They cover:

- The participation strategies adopted by partnerships and the 'rules of the game'
- The structure, culture and management of partners' own organisations and the extent to which these allow them to engage with and respond to communities (the 'capacity' within partners)
- The organisational capacity within communities

These three areas form the core of the audit tools. They are followed by a short section on outcomes.

In each area, there are a small number of questions that the audit needs to address. Each question is followed by a short paragraph explaining why it is important and stating the indicator that the response would provide. These are summarised below:

There are many more issues that could be audited under each heading, but it is important to start with a process that is manageable. The attached tools are intended as a starting point only, drawing attention to some of the key issues. The

tools will be piloted and will need to be customised for local use, drawing on the ideas and priorities of local communities and other partners.

How to measure it

For each of these questions, there is a 'tool' or 'appraisal exercise'. There are three main types of audit tool:

1. Baseline mapping exercises to establish the context within which participation is being introduced
2. Checklists of:
   - activities or approaches that contribute to effective community involvement;
   - questions that need to be asked if community involvement is to be effective
3. Scales to help stakeholders think through the quality and extent of the participation activities that they are putting in place

Some of the questions require **statements of fact,** which can be used to make assessments of participation at different points in the development of a partnership, but many (especially the checklists and scales) require **subjective judgements,** because they are difficult to measure in any objective way. These judgements may vary between partners and communities.

A fourth type of tool, which applies only to outcomes, is a 'decision trail' to track:

- how and whether selected items raised by communities get onto the decision making agenda;
- how these items are eventually decided – and by whom;
- how the decision was reported back to the various partner organisations and communities;
- what happened to the decision en route to implementation;
- if and how it was implemented and by whom;
- how it was monitored.

The decision trail can be used in two ways. It can start with an item that a local community puts on the partnership agenda which can be tracked through the decision-making process to see whether it is implemented or blocked. Using a decision trail would be like putting dye in the system and seeing where it flows through and where it gets blocked. Alternatively, the decision trail can start with a decision that has clearly come out of the partnership and track back to where it came from. This is equally important: it is important for partners to be prepared to ditch cherished top-down plans that local communities do not see as a priority; it is also important that communities as well as partners are creating the agenda for partnership.

What the measures offer

The tools are designed to:

- identify the elements that make for effective partnership with communities – the issues that agencies and communities in partnerships need to think about;
- identify the options that are available for effective community participation;
- identify where there is room for improvement;
- identify where there is already good practice to build on;
- offer external validation.

They give participants in partnership some criteria with which to engage in debate, but they can be customised to the local situation. Their purpose is

to act as an aid to analysis, debate and learning within the partnership. The intention is that they should give partnerships the tools to:

- develop a strategy;
- assess their progress over time;
- compare different experiences and perceptions within the partnership;
- learn together about what works and what does not;
- benchmark against other partnerships.

For example, those tools that require subjective judgements provide an opportunity to compare and contrast the perceptions of different stakeholders. Thus, asking 'What is the balance of power within the partnership?' will show whether different stakeholders have different views on this subject. It will also provide the basis for discussion about the evidence on which these views are based. The extent to which different stakeholders make different judgements may change over time, with more agreement as and when power is shared more widely. It would also be useful to repeat the preliminary mapping exercises later in the process to assess whether participation in the partnership has had any impact on community participation more generally.

Who does the audit?

The exercises can be used as a self-assessment tool, but we suggest that they will be most effective if there is an outside facilitator, especially if they are to be used for external validation. The most effective way of providing this facilitation would be through peer audit, using teams of experienced community representatives and community professionals from other regeneration areas. These teams would be trained in the use of these tools, perhaps with the support of researchers or consultants with relevant experience. Such teams could form a Community Participation Audit Commission, which would develop the tools further to ensure that they promote good practice and support those who are committed to making participation work. Some consideration would need to be given to how to fund such teams, but if regeneration funders are serious about community participation, an investment in audit might be a good way of ensuring that the rhetoric becomes reality.

The audit process

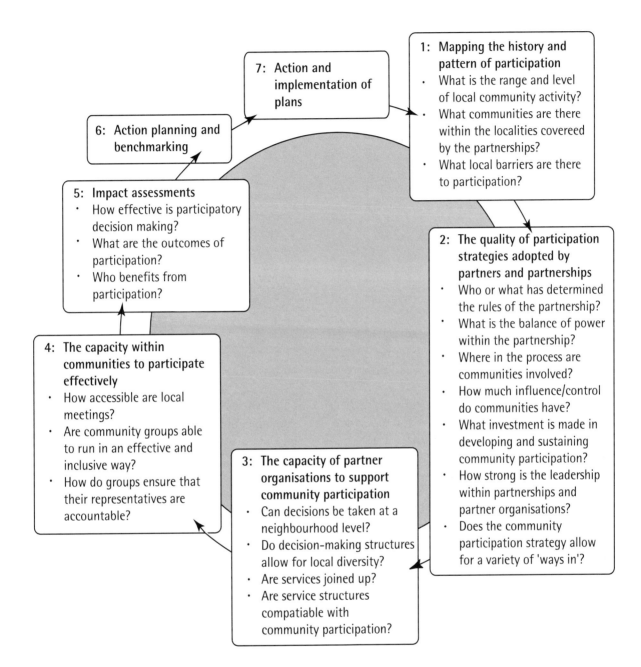

7: Action and implementation of plans

6: Action planning and benchmarking

5: Impact assessments
- How effective is participatory decision making?
- What are the outcomes of participation?
- Who benefits from participation?

4: The capacity within communities to participate effectively
- How accessible are local meetings?
- Are community groups able to run in an effective and inclusive way?
- How do groups ensure that their representatives are accountable?

3: The capacity of partner organisations to support community participation
- Can decisions be taken at a neighbourhood level?
- Do decision-making structures allow for local diversity?
- Are services joined up?
- Are service structures compatiable with community participation?

1: Mapping the history and pattern of participation
- What is the range and level of local community activity?
- What communities are there within the localities covereed by the partnerships?
- What local barriers are there to participation?

2: The quality of participation strategies adopted by partners and partnerships
- Who or what has determined the rules of the partnership?
- What is the balance of power within the partnership?
- Where in the process are communities involved?
- How much influence/control do communities have?
- What investment is made in developing and sustaining community participation?
- How strong is the leadership within partnerships and partner organisations?
- Does the community participation strategy allow for a variety of 'ways in'?